BFI Film Classics

C000112856

The BFI Film Classics is a series of books that introduces, interprets and celebrates landmarks of world cinema. Each volume offers an argument for the film's 'classic' status, together with discussion of its production and reception history, its place within a genre or national cinema, an account of its technical and aesthetic importance, and in many cases, the author's personal response to the film.

For a full list of titles available in the series, please visit our website: www.palgrave.com/bfi

'Magnificently concentrated examples of flowing freeform critical poetry.'
Uncut

'A formidable body of work collectively generating some fascinating insights into the evolution of cinema.'
Times Higher Education Supplement

'The series is a landmark in film criticism.'
Quarterly Review of Film and Video

La Grande Illusion

Julian Jackson

palgrave
macmillan

A BFI book published by Palgrave Macmillan

First published in 2009 by
PALGRAVE MACMILLAN

on behalf of the

BRITISH FILM INSTITUTE
21 Stephen Street, London W1T 1LN
www.bfi.org.uk

There's more to discover about film and television through the BFI. Our world-renowned archive, cinemas, festivals, films, publications and learning resources are here to inspire you.

Palgrave Macmillan in the UK is an imprint of Macmillan Publishers Limited, registered in England, company number 785998, of Houndmills, Basingstoke, Hampshire RG21 6XS. Palgrave Macmillan in the US is a division of St Martin's Press LLC, 175 Fifth Avenue, New York, NY 10010. Palgrave Macmillan is the global academic imprint of the above companies and has companies and representatives throughout the world. Palgrave® and Macmillan® are registered trademarks in the United States, the United Kingdom, Europe and other countries.

Series cover design: Ashley Western
Series text design: ketchup/SE14
Images from *La Grande Illusion*, Réalisations d'Art Cinématographique; posters on pp. 97, 98 courtesy of Iconothèque de la Cinémathèque française; *La Chienne*, Établissements Braunberger-Richebé; *Pépé le Moko*, Paris Film Production; *La Vie est à nous*, Parti Communiste Français; *Casablanca*, © Warner Bros.; *Tire au flanc*, Néo Film; *Boudu sauvé des eaux*, Productions Michel Simon; *Le Déjeuner sur l'herbe*, Compagnie Jean Renoir.

Set by Cambrian Typesetters, Camberley, Surrey
Printed in China

This book is printed on paper suitable for recycling and made from fully managed and sustained forest sources. Logging, pulping and manufacturing processes are expected to conform to the environmental regulations of the country of origin.

British Library Cataloguing-in-Publication Data
A catalogue record for this book is available from the British Library

ISBN 978–1–84457–285–4

Contents

Acknowledgments

I was able to present some of the ideas in this book to seminars in the
History Departments of Cardiff, Queen Mary and Southampton
universities, and I am grateful for the many helpful comments I
received. Kevin Passmore of Cardiff University has provided me with
some useful references which I did not know about and our
discussions about the film (which he unaccountably likes less than I
do) have proved very stimulating. Christophe Dupin, formerly of
Queen Mary History Department, and now at the BFI, has been
hugely generous with advice and references. Geoffrey Nowell Smith
was kind enough to read the manuscript through and save me from
some errors. Patrick Higgins also read the manuscript and offered, as
always, many insights. Finally, I dedicate this book to my former
colleague, once Head of Department, and now good friend, Dick
Shannon, because it was with him that I first saw the film in Paris in
(I think) the summer of 1985. We have often discussed the film over
the years and share the same admiration for it.

Introduction: Paris 1937

In the spring of 1937 the eyes of the world were on Paris, where a huge international exhibition had opened at the start of May. France's left-wing Popular Front government hoped this would be a chance to showcase its achievements to the world. The Popular Front believed in peace, progress and freedom, but the reality of Europe in 1937 was very different. In the previous year, civil war had broken out in Spain, and one highlight of the Exposition was Picasso's denunciation of war, *Guernica*, exhibited in the Spanish pavilion. Another spectacular feature were the pavilions of the Soviet Union and Nazi Germany, standing directly opposite each other. The Nazi pavilion was surmounted by a huge eagle carrying a swastika in its claws which towered above the Soviet pavilion crowned by two massive statues of a worker and a peasant woman striding into the socialist future. This seemed an eerie premonition of future war. The left's dreams of peace were cruelly mocked by the imminent reality of war.

There could have been no more appropriate setting for the launching of Jean Renoir's famous film about war and peace, *La Grande Illusion*. The film opened at Paris's Marivaux cinema on 9 June 1937. It was an immediate triumph, becoming one of the most significant cultural events surrounding the Exposition. In that cinema alone 200,000 spectators saw it in two months and it ended as the highest-grossing film of the year. As well as this popular success, the film attracted universal critical acclaim. This is particularly remarkable given the violent political conflicts tearing France apart at this time. Although *La Grande Illusion* treated controversial political issues, with few exceptions it was greeted enthusiastically by critics across the political spectrum – communists and fascists, pacifists and nationalists, anti-racists and anti-Semites. The film also had a huge international impact, although its reception abroad was less unanimously favourable than in France. It was denounced in Nazi Germany and in fascist Italy, despite winning a special prize for 'best artistic ensemble' at the 1937 Venice Film Festival – a category invented because Mussolini was unhappy that it should win the top prize which was named after him. A special showing was laid on at the White House for Eleanor Roosevelt's birthday in October 1937. Franklin Roosevelt publically endorsed the film, declaring that 'all democrats in the world should see this film'. In 1938, it was the first foreign film ever nominated for an Oscar, before the invention in 1947 of the foreign film category. Although it did not win the Oscar, the film ran for six months in New York, going on to win a special critics' prize at the New York World Fair of 1939. When Renoir went to the USA in 1941, Hollywood welcomed him as the director of *La Grande Illusion*. The film's success has also proved enduring. At the Brussels World Fair in September 1958, a panel of 117 film critics from twenty-six countries voted it the fifth-greatest film ever made.[1] Every time it was revived in France after the war, it continued to fill cinemas.

Such overall and enduring success is unusual. How many other films have achieved both such immediate critical and popular success, and continued to do so sixty years later? Who now remembers the other commercial successes of French cinema in 1937: the military vaudeville *Ignace*, *Double crime sur la ligne Maginot*, *Trois artilleurs au pensionnat*, *Marthe Richard au service de la France* (in which one star of *La Grande Illusion*, Erich von Stroheim, also performed)? The other Renoir film of the 1930s now generally considered an artistic masterpiece, *La Règle du jeu*, was a flop on its release in 1939. It had to await the 1960s before achieving celebrity, and it remains probably more an art-house film than one as genuinely loved as *La Grande Illusion*. In the autumn of 2008, while on a train to Blois, I overheard a group behind me discussing their favourite war films. Their knowledge was encyclopaedic but when someone exclaimed, 'Of course, there is also *La Grande Illusion*,' there was a collective sigh of enthusiasm until another one corrected him: 'Ah yes, but *La Grande Illusion* is different; it is so much more. It is all France of the 1930s.' The discussion of war films was replaced by a long exchange of their favourite moments from this film which clearly formed as much part of their artistic patrimony as Alexandre Dumas. When the historian Jay Winter was involved, during the 1990s, in setting up a museum of the Great War at Péronne in northern France, he contacted surviving veterans to ask what films they would like included in the museum's collection. Three replied directly to his request – in each case choosing *La Grande Illusion*.[2]

The extraordinary success of *La Grande Illusion* raises problems of interpretation. The film may now be considered a 'timeless' classic, but when making it Renoir was closely associated with the French Communist Party and, whatever the film's universal appeal, it was also addressing specific preoccupations of France in the 1930s. Does that mean that we now read the film differently from Renoir's intentions or from the way it was read by his contemporaries? Probably the most common description of *La Grande Illusion* today is that it is a 'pacifist film'. Is it, however, a pacifist film that people thought they were seeing in 1937? Were all people in 1937 indeed seeing the same film? How is it possible that when French politics was in a state of latent civil war, the film could have been so universally praised? Was this unanimity the result of misunderstandings? Quite apart from the film's 'message', what qualities made it so commercially successful? It is certainly an easier film to appreciate than *La Règle du jeu*, but how are its effects achieved? Renoir had already established a considerable reputation, and *La Grande Illusion* was his twentieth film, but he had never previously enjoyed such box-office success (and never did so again).

In answering these questions, we are offered guidance by Renoir himself, who made numerous comments about his films over the years. But his statements cannot always be taken at face value. From the 1950s, Renoir came to be idolised by the young critics of the *Cahiers du cinéma*. They produced a compelling interpretation of the kind of film-maker they believed Renoir to be, stressing purely cinematic qualities of his work over its ideology. Flattered by this adulation, Renoir himself came to believe their version of his career: when the late Renoir talks, it is sometimes the early *Cahiers du cinéma* that is speaking. In reaction against this tendency, from the 1960s other critics began offering contextualised readings of Renoir's work, locating it in the politics of the 1930s. For a film like *La Grande Illusion*, which was so clearly tackling political themes, this is clearly a salutary development, providing it is informed by sufficient sensitivity to the complexities of the period.

Before anything else, however, we must begin by situating the film in the context of Renoir's previous life. Renoir wrote in his autobiography of his suspicion of the idea of the artist as individualist, and his conviction that 'every human being, whether or not he is an artist, is largely a product of his environment'.[3] Examining this environment is especially important when analysing *La Grande Illusion* since it drew more than any of his previous films on his own personal experiences.

1 Renoir before *La Grande Illusion*

Jean Renoir was the middle son of the painter Auguste Renoir.
He was born on 15 September 1894 in the Paris district of
Montmartre, which still had the atmosphere of a bohemian artistic
village. What influence did these origins have on his own artistic
sensibility? He wrote towards the end of his life that, 'I have spent my
life trying to determine the extent of the influence of my father upon
me.'[4] In 1962, he published an affectionate memoir of his father
drawing on long conversations they had had in 1915, just after the
death of Jean's mother, when they were both cooped up in Auguste's
Paris apartment – the latter immobilised by arthritis and his son by a
war injury – when Renoir claims first to have got to know his father
rather than seeing him through a child's eyes. He portrays him as a
sort of conservative anarchist who despised politicians, and refused
to take sides in the Dreyfus Affair. Suspicious of intellectualism,
he preferred to see himself as an artisan of paint than an artist.
As remembered by his son, Auguste detested progress, science and
the bourgeois world of money-making. His particular *bêtes noires*
included the bleakly uniform Paris of Haussmann and the pomposity
of the Opera Garnier. Renoir recalls his father musing already in
1915 that the war was the end of a world.[5]

  Renoir my Father was written when Jean Renoir himself was
disillusioned about the modern world. It is suffused with nostalgia
about his *belle époque* childhood, to which he returned in his later
films such as *French Cancan* (1955) or *Elena et les hommes* (1965).
In his own film autobiography twelve years later, his opinions sound
identical to his father's. While one must not necessarily read this
postwar Renoir back into the 1930s, *La Grande Illusion* certainly
displays a fascination with the vanished world represented by the
military career officers von Rauffenstein and de Boëldieu. Similarly in

his next film, *La Marseillaise* (1938), ostensibly a committed work celebrating the French Revolution, the elegiac portrait of Louis XVI (played by Renoir's brother) lingers in the memory more than the revolutionary heroes. Even in his most politically 'progressive' period, Renoir seems very much his father's son.

In 1913, Renoir enlisted in the cavalry. The choice was influenced by his father, who had served in the cavalry during the Franco-Prussian War, but it also reflected the romantic adventurism characteristic of young men of his generation. In the 1960s Renoir wrote a novel about a French cavalry officer, drawing on his own experiences. At one point the hero recalls: 'I still feel stirring of the blood at the memory of my finest moment as a cavalryman, the charge by the whole division which was the highpoint of the manoeuvres.'[6] Renoir's adolescent dreams of military adventure were shattered by the outbreak of a war different from what anyone had imagined. To experience the thick of the action, he joined the infantry of the Chasseurs Alpins until being badly injured in April 1915. The wound turned gangrenous and only the intervention of Renoir's mother prevented the doctors from amputating his leg. Renoir pulled through, but limped for the rest of his life.

After recovering, Renoir signed up for the air corps, partly because it did not require a medical examination for entry and possibly because it also embodied something of the glamour of the cavalry: fighter pilots were celebrated as 'knights of the sky'. It is striking that the two main French protagonists of *La Grande Illusion*, Captain de Boëldieu and Lieutenant Maréchal, are respectively from the cavalry and the air force. It was in an aeroplane that Renoir first used a camera professionally, photographing enemy positions. The opening scene of *La Grande Illusion*, when Maréchal is asked to fly de Boëldieu on an air reconnaissance mission, was directly inspired by Renoir's own memory of the war. Unlike them, Renoir was never shot down, but on one occasion he came close when his twin-engine wooden plane was fired upon by a faster German one. Renoir was saved by a French pilot flying a more modern Hispano-Suiza.

That pilot, Major Pinsard, was, we shall see, to play his own part in the origins of *La Grande Illusion* twenty years later. Renoir was injured in a flying accident in 1917, and he spent the rest of the war deskbound in Paris. One does not have the impression that Renoir found his war experiences particularly traumatic, or that the enthusiasm with which he entered the cavalry in 1913 had turned into anti-militarism. In 1928 he made a mildly satirical military vaudeville, *Tire au flanc*, whose vision of army life is not unaffectionate.

After the Armistice, Renoir set up as a ceramicist on the advice of his father, who had started out the same way before becoming a painter. Auguste died in 1919, leaving his three sons financially independent. For a while Jean continued producing pottery, but in 1924 he suddenly decided to try his hand at making films. His love of cinema had been ignited in 1916 when the films of Chaplin hit France. Renoir became a fanatical cinemagoer, claiming sometimes to have seen 200 films a month. His passion was American cinema, since he found French films too imitative of the theatre. Renoir had two cinematic epiphanies in this period. The first was seeing in 1923 *Le Braiser ardent* (*The Burning Brazier*) by the Russian immigrant director Ivan Mosjoukine. Renoir claimed that this film proved to him that good films could be made in France. His second moment of revelation was Erich von Stroheim's film *Foolish Wives* (1922), which he had soon watched over ten times. Writing in 1938, the year after *La Grande Illusion*, Renoir explained what von Stroheim had taught him:[7]

Something simple I had not known, that a Frenchman who drinks red wine, and eats Brie, against a grey Parisian vista, can only create a work of merit if he draws on the tradition of people who have lived like him. After *Foolish Wives* I began to look. It astounded me ... I glimpsed the possibility of making contact with the public by the projection of authentic subjects in the tradition of French realism. I began to look around me and, amazed, I discovered many things purely French quite capable of transposition to the screen. I began to see that the gesture of a laundress, of a woman combing her hair before a mirror, of a street pedlar in front of his cart, often had an

incomparable plastic value. I made again a sort of study of French gesture in
the paintings of my father and the artists of his generation.

The importance of 'realism' and the need to make films 'in a
national tradition' seem curious lessons to learn from the film of an
Austrian émigré director using reconstructed sets of Monte Carlo in
Hollywood, but Renoir was certainly influenced by von Stroheim's
filming techniques, in particular his use of *plan séquences* – long-held
shots where the action occurs through movement within one frame
rather than by cutting together different shots.

The catalyst for Renoir's move from watching films to making
them was to create a showcase for his wife Andrée, who had been his
father's last model. Under her acting name of Catherine Hessling, she
starred in five films made by Renoir in the 1920s. Film historians pore
over Renoir's early films to detect the film-maker that he would become,
but had they not been made by Renoir it seems unlikely that anyone
would remember these films today. In total Renoir made nine silent

Foolish Wives: realism *à la* von Stroheim

films between 1924 and 1929, experimenting with different genres and also assembling a team of associates who would stay with him in many of his later films. This often gives his films the feel of ensemble pieces, even family affairs (after all, he had started out making films for his wife). Many people who participated in *La Grande Illusion* had worked with Renoir before. The film's editor, Margueritte Houllé-Renoir, Renoir's partner (although never his wife) after the breakup of his marriage, had worked on five of his previous films; so had the film's assistant director Jacques Becker (who also played the part of an English officer) and the assistant cameraman Claude Renoir, Renoir's nephew. The sound engineer, Joseph de Bretagne, had worked three times previously with Renoir and the set designer, Eugène Lourié, once before. Renoir's brother, Pierre, who had already acted in two of his previous films, was originally to have played one of the German officers until von Stroheim appeared on the scene.

Perhaps because Renoir had not established a distinctive style as a silent film-maker he could adapt to sound more easily than others. For some this was a hurdle to be surmounted, for Renoir an opportunity to be grasped. His first experiment with sound was *On purge bébé* (1931), a farce based on a play by Georges Feydeau. The film is famous for the sound of a real flushing toilet, and marked the start of Renoir's obsessive attention to the use of realistic sound. His next film, *La Chienne* (1931), is probably the first Renoir film that would still be watched today even if he had never made another. The story of a respectable middle-class functionary who becomes obsessed by a semi-prostitute, killing her when he realises she is cheating on him, it is a *Blue Angel* in which the victim takes his revenge. It was followed three years later by *Boudu sauvé des eaux* (1932) where Michel Simon, the lead actor in *La Chienne*, plays a tramp who wreaks havoc in the household of a bookseller who has saved him from drowning. In both these films, Renoir transformed rather conventional boulevard comedies into something more unsettling.

Renoir once remarked that directors only make one film in different ways. If this is true, it is hard to discern from his output before 1934 what that film might be. On the other hand, one can detect recurring themes even if no overarching vision of the world links them together. He liked depicting water, which functioned for him as a symbol of freedom and escape; he was interested in master–servant relationships; he was drawn to transgressive outsider figures like tramps and poachers (there is a poacher in his first film *La Fille de l'eau* (1925), the hero of *La Chienne* ends as a tramp, and Boudu is the most famous tramp in cinema after Chaplin; poachers reappear in *La Bête humaine* (1938) and *La Règle du jeu*). In the same spirit was Renoir's fondness for the figure of the woodland god Pan, representing sexual potency and freedom from the constraints of civilisation (*Tire au flanc, Boudu sauvé des eaux*). His sensibility seems gently anarchistic, playful and whimsical.

Renoir's next film, *Toni* (1934), was a departure from his two previous satires on the respectability of the French bourgeoisie. Set in southern France, it was a story of passion and murder among a group of Italian immigrant workers. Because of its use of location shooting and non-professional actors, the film has been seen as a precursor of postwar Italian neo-realism. Although *Toni* was not politically engaged like *Rome, Open City*, it is not surprising that its treatment of ordinary working lives should have attracted some political attention at a time when, under the impact of the Depression, French politics was moving leftwards.

Renoir's first clearly political film was *Le crime de Monsieur Lange* (1935). It describes how the workers of a print factory form a cooperative after their company goes bankrupt. On the strength of this film, the Communist Party invited Renoir to oversee the making of a propaganda film for the forthcoming elections. The parties of the left, united in the 'Popular Front', won those elections in May 1936, and Renoir was launched as France's most prominent leftwing film-maker. The years between 1936 and 1939, when Renoir made eight films, were his most productive period. *La Grande Illusion* was the fifth of these works.

2 An Escape Story

La Grande Illusion opens in a French army canteen. Lieutenant Maréchal (Jean Gabin), a car mechanic in civilian life, is listening dreamily to a song on a gramophone record, and hoping to visit a local girl called Josephine. Instead, he is told to accompany a haughty staff officer, Captain de Boëldieu (Pierre Fresnay), on a reconnaissance flight behind German lines. The action moves to a German mess where Captain von Rauffenstein (Erich von Stroheim) is celebrating because he has just shot down the French plane containing Maréchal and de Boëldieu. The two Frenchmen are invited to dine with the German officers before being transferred to a POW camp.

De Boëldieu and Maréchal arrive at the camp of Hallbach. They find themselves sharing quarters with four other prisoners: Rosenthal (Marcel Dalio) from a rich Jewish family, Cartier (Julien Carette) a music-hall actor, a school teacher (Jean Dasté) and an engineer (Gaston Modot). Thanks to food parcels which Rosenthal receives from Paris, the prisoners lead a reasonable existence, eating better than their German captors. At night, they dig an escape tunnel, dispersing the excavated soil surreptitiously during the day. Meanwhile they also prepare a theatrical entertainment with costumes sent from Paris.

Just before the prisoners are to put on their show, news comes that one of the forts at Verdun has fallen to Germany. Defiantly they decide the production will go ahead regardless, and they invite the German guards to attend. During the performance, news arrives that Douaumont has been retaken. Maréchal jumps up on stage in excitement and the prisoners launch into a rendition of 'La Marseillaise' until the German guards break up the spectacle and send Maréchal to solitary confinement. He is released just before the tunnel is ready, but the night the prisoners plan to escape they are transferred to another camp.

Months later, having tried to escape from several more camps, de Boëldieu and Maréchal find themselves together again at the camp of Wintershorn. Located in a gloomy castle, this camp is reserved for the most intrepid POWs who have already tried to escape from other camps. Maréchal and de Boëldieu find that their former comrade Rosenthal is a prisoner in the same camp. There is also a professor of Greek, Demolder (Sylvain Itkine), who spends his time translating Pindar. The camp commandant is the same von Rauffenstein who had shot down Maréchal and de Boëldieu. He has subsequently been so badly wounded that he can no longer fight. Von Rauffenstein comes to treat de Boëldieu, whom he sees as his social equal, like a confidant and friend.

The prisoners hatch an escape plan: de Boëldieu will create a diversion while Maréchal and Rosenthal clamber down the castle walls using ropes. On the night of the escape, the prisoners cause a disturbance by playing flutes and banging on saucepans. They are summoned for a roll call. When de Boëldieu's name is called, he does not answer, and suddenly the sound of someone playing a penny whistle is heard. It is de Boëldieu in the rafters. While the guards' attention is concentrated on this apparition, Rosenthal and Maréchal escape. Von Rauffenstein, not understanding what has possessed de Boëldieu, pleads with him to come down. When he refuses, von Rauffenstein reluctantly shoots him. The final scene in the castle shows de Boëldieu on his deathbed in von Rauffenstein's room.

The action shifts to Maréchal and Rosenthal tramping across snow-covered countryside, slowed down because Rosenthal has twisted his ankle. Maréchal becomes increasingly exasperated, the two men quarrel and Maréchal storms off. A few moments later he returns crestfallen, and they hobble on together. They take refuge in the cowshed of a farm. In the morning, the farmer's wife, Elsa (Dita Parlo) finds them and invites them into her house where she lives alone with her little daughter, Lotte (Little Peters). Her husband and brothers have all been killed in the war. The two men spend several days on the farm, and Maréchal and Elsa form a romantic attachment. The little group celebrates Christmas Eve, building a little nativity theatre for Lotte, but once Rosenthal has recovered from his injury, the two men leave. Maréchal promises Elsa he will come back once the war is over.

The last scene shows Maréchal and Rosenthal reaching the Swiss frontier. They say their farewells, before trudging across the snow. The frontier guards are about to shoot until it is clear that the men have crossed the invisible frontier, and are in neutral territory.

3 The Making of the Film: Auteur as 'Ringmaster'

For the critics of *Cahiers du cinéma*, Renoir was a leading exemplar of the director as 'auteur'. Renoir was later happy to subscribe to this idea. His memoir, *My Life and My Films*, opens: 'The history of cinema, above all of French cinema, during the past half-century may be summarized as the war of the *auteur* against the industry. I am proud to have had a share in that triumphant struggle. In these days, we recognize that a film is the work of its *auteur*, just like a novel or a painting.' Those critics who celebrated the 'auteur' in the 1950s were reacting against France's stale 'cinéma de qualité' – the 'well-made film' – more reliant on dialogue than on uniquely cinematic qualities. That was why they rated the legendary films of Marcel Carné below those of his contemporary Renoir because Carné was too dependent on the scripts of Jacques Prévert (*scénariste* of *Quai des Brumes* and *Les Enfants du Paradis*). Prévert did write the script for Renoir's *Le Crime de Monsieur Lange*, which led the critic André Bazin to comment acidly that it was the Renoir film in which dialogue was too obtrusive: 'It often asks you to listen to it for its own sake.'[8]

Regardless of these auteurist interpretations, in 1930s French cinema the writer of the screenplay was often considered as an equal with the director. The *scénariste* of *La Grande Illusion*, the Belgian Charles Spaak (1903–1975), was one of the most celebrated screenwriters of the period who worked with most important directors. He had already written the dialogue for Renoir's previous film, *Les Bas-fonds* (1936), and once Renoir conceived the idea for what was to become *La Grande Illusion* he turned to Spaak for a screenplay. The film is indeed full of memorable lines, and whether or not these 'ask' to be listened to 'for their own sake', they certainly linger in the memory.

Apart from its ahistorical neglect of the *scénariste*, the auterist theory has other limitations. As two eminent film historians remind us, films are 'placed within complex networks of determinants which include their "makers", but also industrial financial constraints, historical circumstances … the presence or absence of stars, generic expectations in their contemporary audiences'.[9] In the case of Renoir, we need to add the semi-collective practice of film-making, which was his hallmark. Often the film which emerged was quite different Renoir's original intentions, and this was especially true of *La Grande Illusion*. Without denying that the film is 'his' we need to explore what kind of 'auteur' he was. Despite his endorsement of the auterist idea quoted above, he usually preferred describing film-makers as artisans, just as he often claimed his father had preferred to see himself as a good porcelain artisan who became a good artisan of painting.

The idea for *La Grande Illusion* went back to December 1934 when Renoir was making *Toni*. Filming was disrupted by the noise of aircraft from a local air force base. When Renoir contacted the base commander to stop the disruption, he was amazed to discover that this officer was the same fighter pilot, now General Pinsard, who had saved him from being shot down in the war. The two men dined together frequently during the making of *Toni*, and Pinsard recounted other wartime adventures. He had been shot down seven times, and seven times escaped captivity. Pinsard's stories gave Renoir the idea for a film, and he asked Spaak to help write a provisional treatment for a scenario. The basic structure of *La Grande Illusion* is already present in this version although it centres more than the final film on the relationship between de Boëldieu and Maréchal. Renoir included details from his own wartime experiences, and Spaak from the memories of his brother who had been a POW. The episode of 'La Marseillaise' was inspired by the scandal caused when Spaak's brother sung the Belgian national anthem during a theatrical performance in his internment camp. Spaak and Renoir also drew upon the war novel *Kavelier Schanhorts* by Jean de Vallières.

The similarities were significant enough for de Vallières to sue Renoir unsuccessfully for plagiarism once the film came out.

For two years Renoir and Spaak hawked their idea around various producers. No one showed any interest because it was felt there had been a glut of war films. One producer complained that the proposal lacked female love interest, to which Renoir replied that women were not present in prisoner of war camps – although ironically the final film did contain a love story. After these disappointments, Renoir temporarily lost interest. Hearing that Spaak had written another scenario for Julien Duvivier about five unemployed workers who win a lottery ticket, Renoir even approached Spaak to see if Duvivier might be ready to swap scenarios. Duvivier replied: 'Your story of soldiers doesn't interest me at all. ... Have you lost your mind?' Duvivier went on to make his film which became the famous *La Belle équipe*, and Renoir returned to *La Grande Illusion*.[10] Renoir's efforts to sell his scenario were boosted when Jean Gabin, who had acted in Renoir's *Les Bas-fonds*, expressed an interest. Gabin, on his way to becoming the greatest star in the history of French cinema, was an irresistible bait for any producer. The scenario was originally entitled the 'Les Evasions du Captain Maréchal', indicating that Gabin was the central character. Finance was procured from a new production company RAC (Réalisations d'Art Cinématographique) and the contract signed on 9 November 1936.

By the time shooting was about to begin at the start of 1937, Spaak and Renoir had made several changes to the scenario of which three successive versions exist.[11] By the second draft, the number of background characters in the first camp had been increased to include what were as yet only called the Actor, the Teacher and the Engineer. The tone of the final version was less dark than the earlier ones. The first contains a harrowing scene where a Breton prisoner who cannot hide his hatred of the Germans is put in solitary confinement for sixty days and returns in such a pitiable state that he is hardly recognisable. Once filming began, several scenes were cut. The first three versions had shown the air battle where Maréchal and de Boëldieu are shot down but for reasons of cost this was cut. A scene showing the two men being transferred in a train to the first camp was also cut, as was a long conversation (appearing from the second scenario) between two German guards pursuing Maréchal and Rosenthal after their escape. These cuts give the final version a much tighter structure: the transitions between scenes are effected with greater economy and elegance.

The most dramatic transformation occurred after a last-minute piece of casting when Spaak was already working on another project: this was the decision to offer a role to Erich von Stroheim. Von Stroheim's Hollywood directing career had long finished because no producers would provide the massive budgets his films required, and he had returned to Europe to relaunch himself as an actor. There are contradictory accounts as to who offered von Stroheim a part in *La Grande Illusion*. Since he was in France to play chief of the German Secret Service in a film about Marthe Richard, a patriotic French spy of the Great War, also being distributed by RAC, the likeliest explanation is that a producer's assistant thought to kill two birds with one stone by also offering von Stroheim one of the German parts in *La Grande Illusion* without having much idea who he was or knowing that he was one of Renoir's cinematic idols. Renoir was initially wary since the only roles for German characters were so insignificant. But he and assistant director Jacques Becker decided to rewrite the script to create him a bigger role. Part of their solution was to conflate the parts of the squadron leader who shoots down the plane at the beginning and POW camp commandant at the end.

There are different accounts of Renoir's first meeting with von Stroheim, and their working relationship. Given von Stroheim's egotistical self-obsession, the most plausible version seems to be that when told he was going to be working for Renoir von Stroheim had no idea who he was and asked to have the name repeated to him. Renoir was initially evasive about von Stroheim's part because he barely knew what it was himself, promising only that it would be 'magnificent'. He and Becker feverishly set about rewriting the script to fit von Stroheim in. This also left the field open to von Stroheim to make his own suggestions. He recalled later:

I had, alas, seen none of his films. But I testified warmly to my enthusiasm at working with him ... I had read the rough scenario that had been communicated to me and I proposed – being incorrigible – a few timid suggestions ... He entered into the subject with an enthusiasm which made tears come to my eyes.

'Timid suggestions' were not von Stroheim's style, and Renoir has a different version:

At the start of the shooting of La Grande illusion Stroheim was quite impossible. We had a quarrel over the first scene in the German canteen. He could not understand why I had not agreed to put what he called Viennese-style whores in the scene. I was beside myself. My idol was in front of me, acting in my film and instead of the oracle from whom I hoped to find the truth, I found someone stuck in the most puerile cliches.

Renoir claimed that he burst into tears and the two men fell into each other's arms, von Stroheim also in tears, and von Stroheim agreed that in future he would follow 'my ideas with the docility of a slave'.[12] This is rather different from von Stroheim's account – except that both figure much histrionics and many tears.

There is no doubt that von Stroheim did contribute significantly to the construction of his part, designing his own costume with its extraordinary neck brace. Von Stroheim was delighted when Eugène Lourié, the set designer, asked him to suggest props he might need. On the next day von Stroheim had a list ready: 'What a list it was. Three type written pages: six pairs of white gloves, a collection of riding crops, five photographs in silver frames of heavy-set blonde Wagnerian singers, the book Casanova's memoirs and more.'[13] If the most important change in the original conception of the film ensued as a result of von Stroheim's unexpected arrival, there were many others. One resulted from the intervention of Albert Pinkévitch, an assistant to the financier Frank Rollmer, who provided the funds for RAC. Renoir became friendly with Pinkévitch when he was acting as an intermediary between with Rollmer while negotiating the contact for *La Grande Illusion*. During the shooting of the film, Pinkévitch, who had originally been destined to become a rabbi, regaled Renoir with stories of Jewish life, and this encouraged Renoir to increase the importance of the Jewish character Rosenthal. In the original scenario Maréchal was to have escaped with a character called Dolette, but now this role was given to Rosenthal (a decision also necessitated by the fact that the well-known actor, Robert Le Vigan, who was to have played Dolette, turned down the role). Pinkévitch was also a irrepressible punner, and Renoir incorporated many of his verbal jokes into the lines of the actor Cartier. The role of the German farmer's wife was increased once the German actress Dita Parlo was hired for it. Originally there was only to have been a passing sexual encounter between the woman and the two Frenchmen on the run, but Parlo was too well-known a star to be given such a minor part.

Other additions to the film occurred for quite circumstantial reasons. While scouting the castle which was the setting for the second camp, Lourié spotted a small geranium in a pot and suggested including it in the set. Renoir agreed and wrote it into the script. When von Rauffenstein is asked why he tends this tiny flower, he replies that 'apart from nettles and ivy it is the only living thing in the castle'. The flower subsequently gives rise to one of the most memorably symbolic moments of the film when the distraught von Rauffenstein cuts it immediately after de Boëldieu's death. It becomes a symbol of von Rauffenstein's grief and the sign of the passing of historical era.

Some modifications to the film occurred after so much discussion that no one was ultimately sure who deserved credit. This is true of Maréchal and Rosenthal's scene in the mountains after escaping. Originally the script had them bound together in solidarity. When Rosenthal's limp jeopardises their escape, he implores Maréchal

to continue alone and save himself. Maréchal agrees but a few
minutes later he cannot bear to go on and comes back to look after his
comrade despite the consequences. In the final version, however, the
two men become increasingly exasperated with each other and have a
violent argument. As Maréchal stomps off, Rosenthal defiantly starts
to sing in a kind of delirium at the top of his voice until he becomes
desperate and exhausted. His singing peters out, just as the contrite
Maréchal returns. Why this change? Dalio claims to have told Renoir
that the original scene did not carry conviction when he tried to play
it. Françoise Giroud, later famous as the founder of the *L'Express*, but
at this time an eighteen-year-old employed to type the changing
versions of the script, says she suggested the modification. As for the
idea of the song, Renoir claims that the weather was so cold that the
two actors could barely speak their lines and so he had the idea of
Rosenthal singing instead – but this is contradicted by the fact that the
song, in the context of the friendly separation of the two men, was
already in the second scenario.[14] It hardly matters who was right, but

the uncertainty reveals much about Renoir's working methods and
how the final version of the film emerged.

In the end, then, *La Grande Illusion* was in many respects
different from the film as originally conceived – so different that
Gabin, although remaining the central character, was unhappy with
the final result, feeling that Renoir had become too taken with the
'Kraut' (von Stroheim). Spaak was so displeased by the changes that
he did not attend the premiere. Renoir wrote him an apologetic
letter: 'You know well this invincible force which pushes me during
the making of a film to turn everything upside down [*chambarder*].
But note that these "chambardements" do not come about from me
alone. I am incapable of working without collaborators – and they
contributed to upsetting the original conception.'[15] As Renoir
wrote on more than one occasion: 'when one makes a film, the
relationships between collaborators – I should almost say
accomplices – become strangely intimate'.[16] From her experience of
working on *La Grande Illusion*, Giroud compared Renoir to

blotting paper, absorbing all influences around him.[17] Over the years Renoir himself employed various analogies to describe his conception of the creative process. He characterised the film-maker as 'not a creator but a midwife', as a ringmaster (*meneur de jeu*) and as a master chef relying upon the assistance of a team of professionals. On another occasion he compared the film-maker to a ceramicist, the activity in which he had started out: 'the ceramicist imagines a vase, makes it, paints it, bakes it – and after several hours he takes out of the oven something completely unexpected, and very different from what he had wanted to make or thought he was making'.[18]

Despite Renoir's capacity for absorption, there was no doubt he did see himself as the film's 'author'. When asked who could be described as the author of a film, he replied: 'the strongest one: around the table are sat a writer, a great star, a director, a producer. Among these men, there is one who will impose on the others an overall conception [*ligne directrice*] without which a work of art cannot exist. That one is in my view the author.'[19] What he said of his father he might equally have said of himself: 'he knew how to let himself be influenced while still remaining himself'.[20]

4 Variations on Realism: 'Interior Truth' and 'Exterior Truth'

This organic and semi-collective process of creation gives *La Grande Illusion* an extraordinary feeling of naturalness even in its more melodramatic moments. Everything in the film seems 'right', 'inevitable'. For the critic André Bazin, whose book on Renoir Truffaut called 'the best film book by the best film critic on the best film director', Renoir was above all an exemplar of 'realism'. But Bazin's definition of realism is so gnomic that his argument becomes circular: what he likes about Renoir is by definition realistic.

'Realism' comes in many forms. One version was the 'poetic realism' of Marcel Carné. But this highly stylised realism is closer to the neo-expressionism of film noir, where nothing is left to chance, everything is shot in studio and the reflection on every wet cobblestone is carefully calculated. There is Italian 'neo-realism' where 'realism' resides in location shooting, the use of non-actors and the subject matter of ordinary people. *Toni* is often seen as a precursor of this style, although Renoir always used 'real' sound whereas in Italian cinema dubbing was the standard procedure. When the subject matter of the film becomes the criterion of 'realism' we are straying more into the territory of 'populism', as in a film like *Hôtel du Nord*. What kind of realism does Renoir offer us?

What Renoir claimed he deplored in French 1920s film-making was its theatrical artificiality as opposed to American films of the same period. He talks of his 'dreams of uncompromising realism' in the 1930s,[21] but what exactly did he mean by this, and how were the effects created? One answer lies in Renoir's concern with authentic detail, such that he even had Gabin wear his own old aviator's jacket in the first scenes. For advice on the German scenes Renoir solicited the advice of his German friend, the art historian, Carl Koch, husband of Lotte Reiniger, a pioneer of silhouette theatre. Once when Renoir and Koch were exchanging reminiscences about the war, they realised that they had been opposite one another on the front near Reims. Described as a 'technical adviser' in the credits of *La Grande Illusion*, Koch was required to verify the authenticity of the details of German military life. On one occasion this caused a bust-up with von Stroheim: 'Koch had a dispute with Stroheim about the over-elaborate clothing of the actress playing the part of the nurse. The argument became heated with Stroheim defending the artist's right to transform reality, and Koch replying that Stroheim had not fought in the war and should therefore keep his mouth shut.'[22] Von Stroheim accused Koch of being petty bourgeois and threw a glass at him. Koch was probably right about the nurse (though, seeing how she appears in the film, he probably lost that argument), but even he missed some details. When the film came out, Renoir was contacted

by a spectator to point out it would have been impossible for von Stroheim to shoot de Boëldieu at such a distance with the revolver he was using. Such details delighted Renoir, and he was intrigued enough to contact the letter's author, Antoine (Tony) Corteggiani, who had an encyclopaedic knowledge of military matters. Renoir promptly hired him to supervise the authenticity of the troop movements in his next film, *La Marseillaise*. His obsession with detail knew no bounds.

It was impossible for Renoir to film the exterior scenes of the film in Germany but he did the next best thing by choosing locations in Alsace for the two camps – a barracks in Colmar and the castle of Haut Koenigsburg, both of which had been built by Wilhelm II.[23] For interior scenes shot in studio, Renoir played great attention to the details of the sets. If the 'poetic realism' of Carné owes much to the atmospheric sets of his designer Alexandre Trauner so that one could say, adapting Bazin's remark about dialogue, that they 'draw attention to themselves', almost becoming actors in their own right,

Haut Koenigsburg Castle

in *La Grande Illusion* the details of the sets serve the action. They situate the personalities of the characters like the meticulous descriptions of furniture and clothing in Balzac's novels. In the first two scenes, the French and German canteens are both similar but also subtly different: in the French mess the tables are dispersed and the occupants scattered or at the bar, while in the German one the men all eat at one long table in the centre, gathered around their commanding officer. The similarities suggest these are all men embroiled in a similar conflict, but the differences suggest the contrasting value systems of the two societies. In other cases these details are so unobtrusive that one barely notices them on first viewing the film. In the sleeping quarters in the first camp each man has decorated his sleeping area in a way that reflects his personality and class: the actor has postcards of musical-hall singers, the engineer photographs of dogs, and a row of pipes, Rosenthal reproductions of Botticellis, de Boëldieu pictures of race horses.

Instead of the conventional establishing shot of a new location, Renoir often begins with a close-up of an object which gradually tracks back to reveal a wider picture. The first shot in the film is a close-up of gramophone record playing a popular song, which then pans back to reveal Gabin's head bowed over the record, lost in nostalgia. These close-ups sometimes have a symbolic or proleptic purpose: the scene of de Boëldieu's death opens with the close-up of

French mess; German mess

the crucifix, the Christmas celebration in the farm with a close-up of the manger. In the second camp, we are introduced to von Rauffenstein's material possessions before seeing him. We begin with a close-up of the huge crucifix dominating the chapel where he has his quarters; then the camera moves to a portrait of General Hindenburg, past the single geranium, along a table containing personal effects: a champagne bucket, a bottle, a pistol lying on a leather-bound copy of Casanova's memoirs, a watch, a

Introducing von Rauffenstein

photograph of a woman, a volume of Heine, a nude statuette, binoculars, a bottle of scent with a spray, whips, spurs, swords. This inventory, which speaks of chivalry, rigid Prussianism, hedonism and romantic dandyism, evokes for us the baroquely eccentric personality we are about to meet.

Renoir, however, was under no illusion that dressing Gabin in his aviator's jacket turned him into a convincing pilot. Indeed, his book *My Life and My Films* explicitly scorns the idea that for an actor to play a fisherman it is enough for him to visit a Breton fishing port, join a few fishing trips and purchase some worn clothes: 'After this meticulous preparation, he plays his part, some scenes being shot in Brittany on a real boat. The director does not even use a double for a scene of a real storm. The end of it all is that our actor, unless he is a genius, will seem like a ham.'[24] For Renoir, then, although 'exterior' details were vitally important, nothing mattered more than acting, and the 'rightness' of *La Grande Illusion* derives in large part from the brilliant performances. Of the arrival of sound Renoir commented: 'I had the revelation that what I was most deeply concerned about was character.'[25] His first objective was to make his actors divest themselves of 'fake naturalism' by means of the 'Italian' method, which he had learnt from the actor Louis Jouvet who performed in *Les Bas-fonds* (and was his first choice to play de Boëldieu). On first reading the script, the actors were instructed to speak their lines as tonelessly as if reciting a telephone directory. Renoir wrote: 'When an actor reads a text and puts meaning into it immediately you can be sure it's the wrong meaning ... Its bound to be a cliché, bound to be a banality, because you can't invent anything original right off, so you turn to your filing system, to something you have already.'[26] The actors had to inhabit their roles gradually. But the confrontation between actor and script operated in both directions: 'At the moment of filming a terrifying phenomenon occurs: in the presence of the actors and the settings I realise that all I've done and written is worthless. I realise that a bit of dialogue I thought full of vitality, once said by an actor who brings to it his own personality, is meaningless.' Renoir was ready to adapt a script until the last moment, but this was not so much improvisation as a collective process of revision until the right note was found. The modification of the scene in the snow might serve as an example of this process. 'Great actors', he wrote, 'bring to the surface dreams one has had but had never quite formulated … There arrives a moment when one is no longer oneself responsible for this creation.'[27]

Thus Renoir achieved exceptional empathy with his actors. Gaston Modot, who played the role of the engineer, described Renoir's technique with actors as like a *dressage en douceur* (a gentle breaking in): 'Gently, without seeming to, he dismantles everything and begins all over again. Seduced, the actors purr, stretch, arch their backs under the velvet glove.'[28] Rarely does Gabin display such a range of emotions as in *La Grande Illusion*: the solid honesty of the early scenes, the haggard despair in the isolation cell, the tenderness of his scenes with Elsa. But *La Grande Illusion* was not a star vehicle and it has the feel of an ensemble piece. Apart from Gabin (and the

An ensemble piece I: the prisoners in the first camp greet the new arrivals. From left to right we see Marcel Dalio, Julien Carette, Gaston Modot

special case of von Stroheim), the other established stars were
Fresnay, a classically trained stage actor who had made his cinema
reputation playing the working-class romantic Marius in Pagnol's
Marseilles trilogy, and Dita Parlo, famous in France for her role in
Jean Vigo's *L'Atalante*. In the cases of Dalio and Carette, it was *La
Grande Illusion* that was to turn them into stars. Dalio's only
previous significant cinema role had been a that of a louche police
informer in *Pépé le Moko* (1936). Julien Carette had started as a
music-hall performer and it was after *La Grande Illusion* that he
became a great character actor of French cinema. The fact that they
were not famous before being hired by Renoir should not lead us to
underestimate their contribution to the film. Dalio's memoirs reveal
that he significantly helped to mould the character he was playing,
and the same is surely true of Carette, who, in *La Grande Illusion*,
was able to sing one of his music-hall hits, 'Si tu veux Marguerite …'.

The 'rightness' – the 'reality' of *La Grande Illusion* – emerges,
then, from an alchemy between actors, script and a director. But a final

An ensemble piece II: dreaming of women at home. From left to right we see Gaston
Modot, Jean Gabin, Julien Carette, Jean Dasté, Marcel Dalio

element needs to be added: the camera. Renoir was well known for his particular filming style, which he himself said, with justification, that he employed more successfully than ever before in *La Grande Illusion*. His aim was to achieve an effortless effect of fluidity and naturalism, avoiding fragmentation. He made limited use of montage or of the classic shot/reverse shot alternation, preferring panning and tracking shots with long takes in deep focus. He wrote in 1938: 'the further I go in my profession, the more I'm led to direct in depth relative to the screen ... the more I dispense with those confrontations between two actors placed neatly before the camera as though having their photos taken'.[29] His films have a consistently higher average shot length (ASL) than any other French director of the period.[30] Duvivier's *Pépé le Moko*, which lasts one hour and forty minutes, has 452 shots, while *La Grande Illusion*, which lasts two hours, has 352.[31] For Renoir long takes had the advantage of offering the 'actor a chance to develop his own rhythm in the speaking of his lines'.[32] They also establish a sense of reality because so much action is filmed in temporal continuity.

When the prisoners first arrive in their quarters, the camera moves with them as they (and we) take stock together of their new quarters. In the first meal in the camp, the camera glides over the details of the scene, moving from person to person, while linking them up to each other. Renoir's description of what he achieves in this scene seems absolutely accurate: 'the audience must not notice that the camera is positively dancing a ballet and subtly passing from one actor to another, from one object to another'.[33]

The same ambition to connect the actors to each other and locate them in their environment lies behind Renoir's predilection for shooting in deep focus, linking foreground and background, and also for filming scenes through windows and doors. In his films, and especially in *La Grande Illusion*, we are constantly looking through doors and windows (particularly appropriate for a film about confinement and escape). To do this, Renoir made considerable demands on his designer, Eugène Lourié. The interiors were filmed in studio because the internal spaces of the castle or barracks were not suitable, but whenever Renoir aspired to link interior and exterior scenes through windows he did not want to use unconvincing backdrops for the outside shots, and Lourié was required to find a solution. He recalls:

In Colmar Renoir and I had to devise a scene where our group of prisoners prepare their costumes for their musical spectacle. They are in a second storey room overlooking the yard where young German recruits are exercising (the prison camp is supposedly located in military barracks still occupied by the German army). To show the yard, however, we did not want to use rear projection [which] at this time gave a blinking and unsteady image ... One solution to this problem was to build the entire set for the room on a platform in the middle of the actual barracks grounds, with a window view of the exercises. But building a complete set on location would mean difficult shooting and problems of lighting and sound, so we discarded this idea. Instead we decided to build only the window wall on a platform at the barracks location, from which we could make the point-of-view shot through

Looking through
windows in *La Grande
Illusion*

... and in *La Chienne*

the second floor window. The total scene with the actors would be shot on a four wall set on stage.[34]

A similar solution was employed in another scene starting in the courtyard where the actor is mocking de Boëldieu; then the camera tracks backwards until we realise we have been watching this from a room where the injured Maréchal is having his feet washed by the engineer. Technically, of course, it would have been easier to shoot the first scene in the courtyard, and then cut to the second, but this would have sacrificed the fluid effect for which Renoir was constantly searching.

If in *La Grande Illusion* there is always a lot to see simultaneously, there is also a lot to hear. From his sound engineer Joseph de Bretagne Renoir inherited what he called his 'creed' (*religion*) of authentic sound.[35] He frequently used sound off screen to heighten the effect of naturalism – for example, in the scene described by Lourié above, we also hear the German recruits training

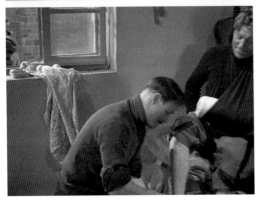

Starting outside and moving inside

in the yard while the prisoners are inside preparing their costumes before the cabaret. This again posed technical problems since the sound of the soldiers marching in a yard could not be easily reproduced in the studio: 'If we had to build stone floors, we had to build them in cellotex, a soundproof material. The actual sound of the steps would be dubbed in later.' Instead, with the help of de Bretange, they used real paving stones: 'they were cast in reinforced cement slabs, heavy to handle but almost indestructible. Twenty years later I saw the same stones still in use at Tobis studies.'[36]

Renoir was always fascinated by popular songs and the dramatic uses that could be made of them, as in the scene in *La Chienne* when we are in the street listening to a song while the murder is being committed inside. Most of the music in *La Grande Illusion*, as often in Renoir films, consists of songs incorporated in the action by being heard or sung by the characters in the film – the song 'Frou Frou' which Maréchal is listening to at the start, the cabaret songs, 'A Long Way to Tipperary' sung by the British, 'Die Nacht am Rein' sung by the Germans, 'La Marseillaise' – except for Joseph Kosma's rather overblown score, which accompanies particularly poignant moments.[37]

These, then, are the means which Renoir employed in his pursuit of 'reality': attention to authentic detail, pushing actors to eschew 'fake naturalism', fluidity of camerawork, naturalistic sound. In the cause of realism Renoir claimed to be prepared to sacrifice formal or classical structure: 'Great works of art are not perfect. Academic works are perfect,' he said in 1963. Or as he put it in his film autobiography: 'nicely constructed works [*la belle charpente*] ... profoundly irritated me'.[38] But this is only part of the story. *La Grande Illusion* is also a very formally constructed film. It divided into three almost equal parts, with a prologue and epilogue, and short transition sequences between each:

Prologue: the two army messes : 7 minutes.
[15-second transition: dissolve to the first camp]

Part One: Hallbach camp: 37 minutes
[1.3-minute transition: dissolve to the second camp]
Part Two: Wintershorn camp: 39 minutes
[6-minute transition: flight of Maréchal and Rosenthal]
Part Three: Farm: 16 minutes
Epilogue in the snow: 3 minutes (2.27)

These three parts are themselves made up of a series of almost self-contained small scenes (eight in the first part, seven in the second). Renoir in 1936 commented on his liking for building films out of small self-contained scenes which could at the end if necessary be modified without jeopardising the architecture of the whole, and that is certainly what he does in *La Grande Illusion* (it is also the way he writes his books).[39] But each of these scenes has its own formal structure and it has been demonstrated by one film historian that they individually replicate the tripartite scheme of the film as a whole.[40] Sometimes the transition between scenes is abrupt but on repeated viewing one becomes aware of recurring themes and motifs, parallels and repetitions – snatches of dialogue, songs, visual echoes – which tighten the structure further: Maréchal listens to the song 'Frou Frou' nostalgically in the first scene and plays it on the harmonica in more tragic circumstances in solitary confinement; the tune de Boëldieu plays on his flute, 'Le Petit Navire', is the same one Rosenthal sings when quarrelling with Maréchal;[41] the engineer washes Maréchal's feet, Elsa washes Rosenthal's; de Boëldieu's comment in the first camp that the German recruits are 'children playing at soldiers' is echoed by von Rauffenstein's in the second: 'My men are not young but it amuses them to play as soldiers'; just before the riot breaks out in the second camp a German guard congratulates himself on being able to keep order because he had been a teacher in civilian life and, in the next scene, witnessing the riot, Demolder remarks how he can now understand why his pupils so enjoyed disrupting classes.[42]

Overlaying its classical tripartite structure, and its pattern of internal echoes, the film has an overall cyclical form. It begins with a

close-up of a black record spinning (before revealing Maréchal who is watching it go round) and ends on a long-distance shot of white snow where two men (Maréchal and Rosenthal) are tiny black dots – heading back presumably from the open space in which they are lost to the confined space in which the film began.

Even if the formalism of *La Grande Illusion* owes something to Spaak,[43] it still remains unexpected from someone claiming to despise *la bonne charpente* over the messiness of reality. This is less surprising, however, if we remember Renoir's equal delight in the artificiality of theatre. Repeatedly he returned to the impact upon him as a child of visiting the Guignol puppet theatre in the Tuileries Gardens. Stages are constantly present in his films: his first major talkie *La Chienne* opens with a miniature theatre, where the real characters we are about to see on the screen are first presented as puppets, as does his last film *Le Petit Théâtre de Jean Renoir* (1969).

Theatricality is omnipresent in *La Grande Illusion*. The prisoners present their tunnel to each other as a piece of theatre, and the tunnel is kept up with props from the theatre. Each of the three parts of the film culminates in a moment of theatricality: in the first, the cabaret; in the third, the miniature nativity. These are both theatres interpolated into the narrative action of the film, but in the second part the theatricality is in the action itself, while de Boëldieu plays his flute with the searchlights trained upon him as if on a stage.

De Boëldieu indeed prepares meticulously for this final performance, carefully washing the white gloves integral to his 'costume'. As he falls to the ground when von Rauffenstein shoots him, he glances at his watch to check the timing of his performance. One could not imagine a more theatrically staged death.

In many other ways the film is highly theatrical. Renoir's repeated use of windows and doors functions not only to link actors to their surroundings, but also frame the action as if through a proscenium arch. His groupings of actors are often very studied – as for example the prisoners arranged at the window listening to the marching in the courtyard below and commenting upon it like a Greek chorus. Although some performances are naturalistic, others are quite the opposite. De Boëldieu was originally to have been played by the famous stage actor Louis Jouvet, and when Fresnay took over the part he found Renoir constantly pushing him towards what Fresnay worried was caricature to 'the limits of excess'.[44] As for von Stroheim, he needed no encouragement to go in such a direction, and his performance is an extraordinary exhibition of flamboyant theatricality. Yet in their own terms these performances ring absolutely 'true'. As David Thomson has written, one of the keys to Renoir is the 'flamboyant action contrasted with the naturalism of the cinematography'.[45]

What Renoir criticised about French cinema when he began making films was its attempt to imitate theatre. His aim was different: to theatricalise cinema. But how does this square with his self-proclaimed obsession with 'realism'? In fact, Renoir's conception of realism was more complex than simple fidelity to authenticity of detail. Frequently he returned to the distinction between what he

Playing at building the tunnel; the Cabaret; de Boëldieu times his last performance, the Nativity

called 'exterior truth' and 'interior truth'.[46] The lesson he claimed to have learnt from von Stroheim in the 1920s was that the artist creates his own reality: 'reality has no value except when it is transposed. An artist only exists if he creates his own little world.'[47] Or as he wrote on another occasion: 'in art, truth, through the transposition of artificial reality … is often most helped by the unreal and the false'.[48] Achieving this inner reality required one to discard the accretions of nineteenth-century bourgeois realism and return to the no less deep 'truth' of the Commedia del Arte (to which he later played homage in his 1953 film *Le Carrosse d'or*): 'Reality is fairytale like [*féerique*]. It requires a lot of patience, work and good faith to find it … You have to eliminate what seems to you to have been created by the habits of your times.'[49]

Perhaps because we are unable to strip ourselves of the 'habits of our times' Renoir's 'interior' truth sometimes seems too whimsical and too personal – but not in *La Grande Illusion*. Truffaut once wrote that it was one of the 'few Renoir films where psychology takes preference over poetry ... it is perhaps the least eccentric [*fou*] of all Renoir's French movies'.[50] This was not meant entirely as a compliment, but perhaps the film works so well because of the balance of poetry and psychology, theatricality and naturalism – a perfect harmony between 'interior' and 'exterior' truth: the truth of Gabin in Renoir's old flying jacket and the truth of von Stroheim in his fantastical costume.

5 Boundaries and Crossing Boundaries

'My chief aim [in *La Grande Illusion*] was the one I have been
pursuing ever since I started to make films – to express the common
humanity of men.'[51] This is certainly one message that anyone will
take from the film. The men in both camps are individuals thrown
together by circumstances – which happen to be war and
imprisonment – through which they discover solidarity: the engineer
washes Maréchal's feet, Rosenthal shares his food with the others.
Yet 'the common humanity of men' is depicted without
sentimentality or any idealisation of the prison camps as some
harmonious community of suffering. The film is as much about what
divides men. As Renoir remarked in a letter in 1937: 'it is not a film
about escapes ... It is a film about the conflicts between men.'[52]
Common humanity *and* conflict.

The two camps operate as a microcosm of the French national
community, but what is striking as the prisoners discover each other
is how separate they remain from each other. In the second camp,
the men remain absorbed in their own activities, semi-indifferent to
each other: Demolder is translating Pindar, a Senegalese soldier is
drawing. When he comes over to show Maréchal his completed
picture, Maréchal looks up distractedly, barely paying attention.
The 'common humanity' of man is always coming up against
obstacles. Maréchal is in constant perplexity about life: 'What is the
"*cadastre*" (land register)?' he asks the engineer; 'Who is "your
Pindar"?' he asks Demolder.

While the film shows Frenchmen discovering what links and
divides them, it is also full of moments of solidarity where individuals
reach across frontiers of language and nationality. In the German
mess, just after the two Frenchmen have been shot down, Maréchal
finds himself sitting next to a German who turns out to speak French

because, like Maréchal, he is a car worker in civilian life and had worked in a factory in Lyon. Maréchal is delighted at this coincidence, and the German offers to cut his meat since Maréchal's arm is in a sling. Later there is the moment when the German guard, trying to comfort Maréchal who has been driven half mad in solitary confinement, offers him cigarettes, discreetly puts a harmonica by his side, then listens at the door enraptured as Maréchal plays a tune on it (the tune 'Frou Frou', which Maréchal had been listening to at the start of the film). Or there is the German guard whom the prisoners nickname 'Arthur', and with whom they form a relationship of teasing complicity.

Renoir often remarked that he believed the 'vertical' frontiers of nationality less important than the 'horizontal' ones of class and this is what many have taken as the central message of *La Grande Illusion*. In truth the film is more ambiguous: sometimes it presents the 'common humanity of men' across national identities, sometimes interactions and conflicts between other kinds of identities. It is about

boundaries and the crossing of boundaries – boundaries of class, of nationality, of gender and of race.

Nation and class

There are four central relationships in the film: between Elsa and Maréchal, Maréchal and Rosenthal, de Boëldieu and Maréchal, Maréchal and von Rauffenstein. Two of these are the most straightforward to interpret. In the first, the decent French worker, Maréchal, and Elsa, the ordinary German farmer's wife, fall in love. They are two individuals brought together by a 'common humanity', and we can read their encounter as class prevailing over nation. The Maréchal–Rosenthal relationship offers the opposite model. They are two men of the same nation, but different classes, thrown together by adversity, and neither sees their social background as an impediment to friendship.

The other two relationships are more ambiguous. De Boëldieu is the one member of the French community whose class keeps him aloof from everyone else. He prefers playing patience to participating in their ridiculous theatrical revue. To the actor's puns he enquires frostily, 'Is that meant to be funny?' When the teacher muses that if he escapes through Holland he will have the opportunity to see tulip fields, de Boëldieu tells him, 'My dear fellow, you have the taste of a parlour maid.' Even when joining their activities, he distances himself with ironic mockery. He agrees to take his turn digging the tunnel because 'people have told me that crawling is marvellous exercise'.

De Boëldieu's icy disdain renders everyone wary of him. To the actor he is 'Mr Monocle'; the engineer initially wonders if should be told about the tunnel. De Boëldieu does know the same Parisian restaurants as the *nouveau riche* Rosenthal, but with Maréchal, who prefers a local bistro 'with a nice bit of plonk' to Maxims, no such affinities exist. On the surface they are divided by an abyss of class. Yet it is between de Boëldieu and Maréchal that a relationship of mutual respect develops, even if neither finds words to express it. Although he has not yet known de Boëldieu for long, Maréchal assures the engineer that he can be trusted: 'Yes, he seems a bit stuck up but he's a good bloke.' De Boëldieu congratulates Maréchal on his idea – 'that's the spirit' (*tres chic*) – that the prisoners should continue their cabaret despite the fall of Douaumont, and even invite the German guards to attend. When it looks as if the prisoners will be escaping from the first camp without Maréchal, who is in solitary confinement, de Boëldieu

Arrival at the camp: bad manners ... and good manners

comes as close to expressing emotion as he seems capable of: 'Yes, I find it a bit depressing too, but that's war … feelings have nothing to do with it.' On the farm, Rosenthal wonders what has come of de Boëldieu but Maréchal finds the thought too painful and brushes it away. Despite this mutual regard, there is always a barrier between the two men. As the escape from Wintershorn draws close, Maréchal tells Rosenthal he is glad to be leaving with him rather than de Boëldieu: 'He's a good bloke, but you can't let yourself go with him … I am not at ease, there is a wall between us … If ever you and I found ourselves in a bad spot, we'd just be a couple of down and outs, while whatever happens to him he's always Monsieur de Boëldieu.' Nonetheless, on the eve of the escape, Maréchal tries to thank de Boëldieu for making it possible:

MARÉCHAL	Listen, for the first time in my life I am really embarrassed.
	[De Boëldieu starts to prepare his plan. Washing his white gloves … Maréchal is trying to thank him]
DE BOËLDIEU	I am not doing anything for you personally. That excuses us from the danger of getting emotional.
MARÉCHAL	There are certain times in life though …
DE BOËLDIEU	Let us avoid them.
MARÉCHAL	You can't do anything like the rest of us. I've been with you every day for eighteen months, and still you say *vous* to me.
DE BOËLDIEU	I say *vous* to my mother and wife …
DE BOËLDIEU [to stop emotion]	A cigarette?
MARÉCHAL	English tobacco tickles my throat. You know, gloves, tobacco … everything comes between us.

The closer the two men are drawn together, the more they become aware of what divides them.

If Maréchal and de Boëldieu cannot find words to express their feelings for each other, the opposite is true of the fourth central relationship: between von Rauffenstein and de Boëldieu. Inasmuch as de Boëldieu has a sustained conversation in the film, it is with von Rauffenstein – most notably in the scene where they pace up and down von Rauffenstein's quarters, to which he has invited de Boëldieu as a privilege. From their first meeting, after von Rauffenstein has shot him down, it is quickly established that he has known de Boëldieu's cousin, Count Edmond, the military attaché in Berlin; they have shared the same girl, Fifi, at Maxims; they reminisce about von Rauffenstein winning the Prince of Wales Cup in 1909 (riding 'Blue Minnie'); they both wear monocles and impeccable white gloves. In short, they share more with each other than de Boëldieu does with any French prisoner or than von Rauffenstein does with the men under his command who find him peculiar ('The chief is a complete lunatic with his pot of flowers').

But there are limits to de Boëldieu's willingness to accept the complicity into which von Rauffenstein tries to draw him. When von Rauffenstein pointedly asks him to swear there is nothing hidden in the room, de Boëldieu asks why he has not asked any others:

VON RAUFFENSTEIN	Hm. The word of honour of a Rosenthal … or a Maréchal.
DE BOËLDIEU	It is as good as ours.
VON RAUFFENSTEIN	Perhaps.

Later in von Rauffenstein's quarters, de Boëldieu returns to the subject of his fellow prisoners, and von Rauffenstein repeats his conviction that despite being officers in name they are of a different breed from him and de Boëldieu. It is striking that in this long dialogue between the two men Renoir, rarely for him, films them in shot/counter shot, as if to emphasise that as well as sharing a bond they are also locked into a dialogue of the deaf. In this scene of two minutes, forty-five seconds, Renoir uses twenty-one shots, and yet a little later for the scene (quoted above) where Maréchal and de

Boëldieu talk before the escape, which lasts two minutes, two seconds, Renoir uses only three shots.[53]

Although Maréchal and de Boëldieu can barely communicate, and although von Rauffenstein is the only individual to whom de Boëldieu talks easily, in the end he forces von Rauffenstein to shoot him so that Maréchal (and Rosenthal) can escape. In this relationship, at least, the 'vertical' frontier of nation triumphs over the 'horizontal' one of class.

Nothing more clearly embodies these complexities than the use of language in the film. The two camps are not merely a microcosm of the French national community, but that community is placed inside a polyglot community of Russians, English and Germans. In an

United by class, divided by the camera

early scene, a Russian prisoner is teaching a French one to conjugate the verb 'to be' in Russian. The fact that everyone speaks their mother tongue, with subtitles to explain their dialogue, was one of the most novel features of the film.[54] This innovation, often regarded as one of the film's most striking examples of realism, also underscores the film's theme of the arbitrariness of frontiers. Because de Boëldieu and von Rauffenstein form a cosmopolitan aristocratic elite sundered by war, they share English as a lingua franca when they reminisce about the past. This affirms their social distinctiveness from everyone around them. When von Rauffenstein begs de Boëldieu to give himself up, he addresses him in English; de Boëldieu replies in English too: 'Damned nice of you Rauffenstein but it's impossible.' Between other characters English is a barrier. When the French prisoners are about to be moved from the first camp, Maréchal rushes over to tell some newly arriving English prisoners (complete with tennis rackets) about the tunnel – but they cannot understand him, and will spend the war in ignorance of the fact that there is a

Divided by class, united by the camera

completed tunnel under their sleeping quarters. (In fact, in the first versions of the scenario the irony of the situation is underlined: the British are seen settling into their quarters and immediately beginning to dig a tunnel without realising they are above an existing one.)

When Maréchal is in solitary confinement he is almost driven mad because he has not heard French spoken for days. The guard who tries to offer solace has no shared language to communicate with him. When Maréchal and Rosenthal reach the farmhouse, it is the cosmopolitan Rosenthal who turns out to be able to communicate with Elsa in German. Maréchal can talk only to the cow (in French): 'You were born in Wurtemburg and me in Paris, but that does not prevent us understanding each other.' But finally, in his attempts to communicate with Elsa and Lotte, Maréchal redeploys in a more tender context the German vocabulary he has learnt in the camp. The first German words they had heard were '*streng streng verboten*' and now Maréchal mockingly chastises Lotte with the same words to warn her that she must not eat the vegetables used to make the characters in the nativity scene. The language learnt in war has now been humanised by love.

Gender

To decode themes of gender in books or films has become the stock-in-trade of modern academia even when the author of the works in

The British arrive ... but cannot understand Maréchal

question would be amazed at this interpretation of their work. In *La Grande Illusion*, however, Renoir himself explicitly points us in this direction during the single most extraordinary moment of the film.

A crate of costumes has arrived for the cabaret which the prisoners are preparing to rehearse. As the men gather eagerly around the box crammed with women's clothes, memories crowd in on them. Lovingly they caress the silk stockings on their faces. Someone suggests that a prisoner should try a costume on, and Maréchal proposes the 'angel face' Maison-Neuve (Geo Foster). While Maison-Neuve dresses up, the camera remains on the others still excitedly unpacking the clothes. Then Maison-Neuve's voice, in a mocking falsetto, is heard off scene (a typical Renoir touch) announcing that he is ready. We cannot yet see him and Maréchal says: 'Let us dream a bit longer. If we look at you we will no longer be able to imagine.' Suddenly the camera pans round to reveal Maison-Neuve gawkily standing in his dress and wig:

MARÉCHAL	You look like a real girl.
MAISON-NEUVE	Don't you think it's *drôle* [weird/funny].
MARÉCHAL (musingly)	*Drôle* ...
ROSENTHAL	Yes, it's *drôle*.

In what seems like an eternity, the camera pans silently across the transfixed faces of the soldiers who are speechless, seemingly bewitched – but whether through bewilderment or awe or nostalgia or shock or desire, it is impossible to know. The spell is broken as Maison-Neuve clambers forward, less an eroticised male than an awkwardly embarrassed one, repeating 'Oui, c'est drôle.'

The scene perfectly exemplifies the anxieties which the war had generated about the destabilisation of gender boundaries. This was an important theme of French 1920s politics when the 'new woman' with shorter hair and shorter skirts was perceived as a challenge and a threat by many men. The 1922 novel *La Garçonne*, depicting this 'new woman', caused a massive scandal and caused its author to be

stripped of his Légion d'Honneur. Renoir situated the origins of the
scene with the costumes, in a personal memory of the war when he
was visited in the military hospital by his sister-in-law dressed in the
new style, with the news his mother had died of diabetes: 'I was so
shocked by this new creature that it took me several minutes to grasp
her terrible message. The girls my fellow soldiers left behind had long
hair.' He remembered one of his fellow patients remarking that such
an outfit might be all right for Paris but not the provinces where he
lived: 'If I find my wife rigged out like that when I get home, I'll give
her a kick in the arse.'[55] In *La Grande Illusion* also, while unpacking

the clothes, the men discuss the women back at home. The actor is amazed that they are cutting their hair short, and muses that, 'It must be like going to bed with a boy.' The teacher worries this new liberty will give his wife ideas; he is sure she is cheating on him. Another is convinced that his wife would not cut her hair short since such fashions are only for tarts. The conversation is cut short by the apparition of Maison-Neuve in his dress.

The first scenario of the film had a more misogynist edge than the final film. In this version the prisoners are housed in a building whose other wing lodges female German workers. The prisoners can only see their legs though the basement window.

Twice a day when the neighbouring workshops are opening and closing, a woman whom they have never seen puts her foot on one of the bars of the basement window. She pulls up her garter with provocative impudence, showing the prisoners her legs, which are very beautiful. One day they can put up with this no more and decide to 'punish the bitch' [garce], grabbing her by the ankle. They all rush forward toward this leg while her co-workers try to pull her free. They take off her shoe, tear off the stocking. They want to touch her fresh and glowing skin. With cruelty Maréchal bites it. She screams out. The men back off and the women collect her.[56]

The last sequence on the farm was also crueller than the final version. Both men share a moment of sexual release with the farmer's wife in the straw before continuing their journey.

Apart from Elsa, there are no women in *La Grande Illusion* (except the nurse and some old German ladies watching the German recruits), but the memory of women – the sense of their absence – is all-pervasive. The film begins with Maréchal hoping to visit 'Josephine' until he has to abandon the idea. In the second camp, when the prisoners' quarters are being searched, Maréchal is absorbed in a book from which he reads an extract aloud: ' "Louise writes to Victor: I am as tired as a girl who has made love 22 nights running." … Think of that.' We are told that in one of Maréchal's escape attempts he had been dressed as woman. Von Rauffenstein, raising an eybrow, affects to find this 'Drôle … très drôle!' (echoing the prisoners' reaction to Maison-Neuve).

MARÉCHAL	Yes, but what was less funny was that an NCO really took me for a woman and I don't like that at all …
VON RAUFFENSTEIN	Really?
MARÉCHAL	I assure you …

While men can only dream about women or dress up as them, the deepest relationship in the second camp is between two men – von Rauffenstein and de Boëldieu – with a distinct undercurrent of homoeroticism on von Rauffenstein's side. Von Stroheim's performance – spraying himself with scent as he goes to meet the prisoners, his quizzical scepticism when Maréchal says 'I don't like that at all' – verges on high camp, suggesting some ambivalence about his sexual identity. Gender anxieties during the war focused not only on the 'new woman' but also the threatened masculinity of men subjected to the indignities of a war which corresponded to no previous images of military heroism – one example being the men who suffered that female complaint of 'hysteria', now labelled 'shell shock'. For some men the war was experienced as an emasculation. This is certainly true of von Rauffenstein, encased in his neck brace, burnt all over – as much a prisoner of his crippled body as the French are his prisoners. As he confesses to de Boëldieu: 'Believe me, I feel nothing but distaste for my present job … I was a fighting man and, now, I am a bureaucrat, a policeman, it is the only way left for me to serve my country … Burnt all over – that is why I wear these gloves … My backbone fractured in two places … Silver strut in my chin, silver knee caps.' Sharing memories of the past with de Boëldieu are von Rauffenstein's moments of greatest emotional intensity. Von Rauffenstein sits at the bedside of the dying de Boëldieu, and it is after his death that he cuts the geranium, as if signifying his life too has ended.

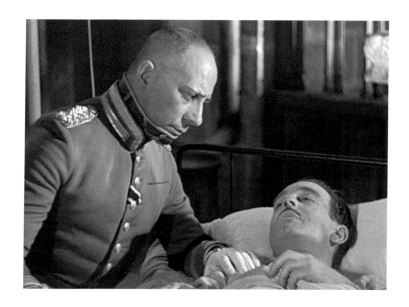

Renoir was aware of these homoerotic undertones. He himself believed in intense male friendships, and wrote of his own close relationship with Becker while making *La Grande Illusion* that 'ill-intentioned people' might have thought that it bordered on 'a relationship of quite another kind'. He commented that the 'Rauffenstein–Boëldieu adventure is nothing less than a love story'.[57] When von Rauffenstein pleads in English (their private language) with de Boëldieu not to force him to shoot – 'I beg you, man to man, come back' – Renoir told him to cry out like a man pleading with his mistress.

After the portrayal of gender disorder in Part One, and the current of homoeroticism in Part Two, Part Three restores heteronormativity in the relationship between Maréchal and Elsa: man, woman and child. Maréchal cuts wood outside while Elsa prepares food inside. As the men are about to leave, her emotion spills out: 'I was alone for such a long time … I had stopped waiting. You will never know the joy it gave me to hear a man's footsteps in this house again.'

Gender normality restored

Race

In 1951 Renoir introduced a screening of *La Grande Illusion* at
Berkeley University, saying that it was the first time he would be
seeing the film with English subtitles. At the end, however, Renoir
'charged down the aisle like an enraged bull' to protest at the
translation of Maréchal's last words to Rosenthal. The subtitle had
read: 'Goodbye old pal' whereas the French words are '*Au revoir sale
juif*' ('Goodbye dirty Jew').[58]

This anecdote reveals the importance for Renoir of the theme of
Jewishness in the film. Anti-Semitism, a feature of French rightwing
politics since the late nineteenth century, had reached new intensity in
the 1930s with the arrival of Jewish refugees from Germany after
1933 and the election of the socialist Leon Blum as Prime Minister in
1936. During the 1930s explicitly Jewish characters were not
common in cinema, although there were often various shady foreign
types (*méteques*) with some Jewish connotations.[59] Marcel Dalio
(born Israel Moshe Blauschild) was quite a specialist in these sorts of
roles – like his snivelling police informer in *Pépé le Moko*, the part
for which he was probably best known before his appearance in *La
Grande Illusion*. Viewers might well have thought they knew what
they were going to find again.

Remarkably, the word 'Jew' does not appear in the film until near
the end, but long before it is uttered Rosenthal has become, in the
words of one commentator, the 'depositary of an accumulation of
Jewish attributes'.[60] Early on we learn that he is from a rich banking
family, that he works in the clothing industry and that his father is
Polish. This makes him the synthesis of two different Jewish
stereotypes, since the East European immigrant Jews working in the
garment trade were not usually rich, and socially distinct from French
Jewish banking dynasties like the Rothschilds. Rosenthal is generous in
sharing his lavish food parcels with his fellow prisoners but this also sets
him apart from them. The teacher, remarking that he has never eaten so
well before, comments drily: 'I am beginning to accustom myself to
Rosenthal's generosity, which shows how adaptable human beings are.'

If the prisoners are clearly aware of Rosenthal's difference, none explicitly makes any comment about the supposed racial characteristics of Jews. The only racial theorising comes from Rosenthal himself when Maréchal comments on his generosity: 'You know it's partly vanity. I am very proud to come from a rich family. When I invite you to dine with me, it gives me the opportunity to prove it to you. People think our worst defect is avarice, but they are wrong. We are often generous because we suffer from the sin of pride.' It is significant in the light of 1930s politics that the only character revealing what seems like open racial disgust is the German von Rauffenstein when the prisoners' quarters are being searched. Alighting upon Demolder's copy of Pindar, he examines his skull briefly before uttering the words 'Poor Pindar' – presumably a suggestion that he (although not Jewish) is a racially debased type not worthy of a great poet representative of Europe's classical tradition (a double irony since von Stroheim was the son of a Jewish hat merchant from Vienna). If this moment seems sinister, the prisoners do also reveal racial assumptions, albeit in more humorous

Marcel Dalio in *Pépé le Moko*

form, during the scene where each explains why they want to escape and their conceptions of patriotism. When it comes to Rosenthal, the actor jokes: 'Oh, him he's born in Jerusalem.'

ROSENTHAL   Sorry. I was born in Vienna, capital of Austria, of a Danish
            mother and a Polish father, naturalised French.
MARÉCHAL   Old Breton aristocracy!
ROSENTHAL   Possibly. But the rest of you, French from way back, you don't
            own a hundred square metres of your country. Well, the
            Rosenthals have managed in thirty-five years to acquire three
            historical chateaux with hunting grounds, lakes, fields,
            orchards, rabbit warrens, fishing rights, pheasants, stud farms
            ... and three picture galleries full of ancestors ... So don't you
            think it is worth escaping to defend all that?

De Boëldieu responds caustically: 'I had never considered patriotism from that particular point of view.'

Von Rauffenstein as phrenologist?

Although no one in this scene offers any more conventionally honourable forms of patriotism, Rosenthal here fulfils another anti-Semitic stereotype: the nouveau-rich Jew buying his way into the old order.

At the same time, however, as presenting this condensation of anti-Semitic stereotypes, Renoir also progressively introduces small touches which humanise Rosenthal and win him sympathy. He generously shares his food; he brushes away a tear when Maréchal returns from solitary confinement; his patriotism is demonstrated by the fact that he first hatches the escape plan in the second camp. In the second camp de Boëldieu and Maréchal seem delighted to meet him again, and he seems more a member of the community than in the first camp – more indeed than de Boëldieu, who is always slightly apart. On the eve of the escape, as we have seen, Maréchal is much happier to be leaving with Rosenthal than he would have been with de Boëldieu. He dismisses Rosenthal's speech about the racial characteristics of the Jews: 'That's just talk. All I see is that you have been a good pal to me.'

Rosenthal hides his emotion (note his Botticelli posters)

This is the point we have reached – Rosenthal's Jewishness being of no importance – when suddenly the word 'Jew' explodes in his quarrel with Maréchal:

MARÉCHAL   Clumsy oaf. We've got nothing else left to eat. We might as well give ourselves up.

ROSENTHAL   Willingly, because I'm fed up too. Fed up. Fed up. Fed up. If only you knew how I loathe you.

MARÉCHAL   Believe me. It's mutual. ... You are a ball and chain tied to my leg. I never could stand Jews for a start, get it?

ROSENTHAL   It is a bit late to discover that ...

But only moments later a contrite Maréchal returns, ready to jeopardise his escape by refusing to abandon his Jewish comrade. This one expression of overt anti-Jewish prejudice in the film is immediately redeemed; it is a moment of exorcism, a reflex insult which belies the bond between the two men. Once they are on the farm, even if Rosenthal is an observer of the relationship between Maréchal and Elsa, it is Elsa who washes his feet, and it is Rosenthal who organises the Christmas ceremony around the manger and with playful irony describes Jesus as his '*frère de race*' and brings himself into the Christian community. So Maréchal's '*sale juif*', almost the last words of the film, represent the end of his journey of

Quarrel; reconciliation

understanding, and perhaps a self-critical reference to his earlier
outburst.

Renoir's strategy in *La Grande Illusion*, then, is not so much to
portray a Jew who does not conform to anti-Semitic stereotypes as to
draw viewers into a dialogue with that stereotype. The figure of
Rosenthal was commented upon by many observers. The communist
critic Georges Sadoul suggested it might have been preferable to
make the rich character a Catholic rather than, more obviously,
a Jew, but it could be argued that if Renoir had not presented a
character whom viewers would recognise as Jewish, he would have

Lotte, Elsa, Rosenthal and the baby Jesus

less effectively challenged their assumptions about how such a character might behave. One writer who certainly saw what Renoir was trying to do was the violently anti-Semitic novelist Louis-Georges Céline, who saw the film as an example of 'Yiddish colonisation'. The Jews 'emerge from the shadows … to centre stage'. Rosenthal starts out as the 'exact condensed product of this abominable class … The absolute parasite, the threatening super Jew, the most contemptible and hateful example of vampiric capitalism' only to be transformed 'into a little neo-Jesus Christ'.[61] Overall the film was an example of 'Mongolo-Yiddish' ideology. Renoir could have received no greater compliment.

Of course, one cannot know how Rosenthal was perceived by most viewers of the film or indeed whether Renoir was entirely free of assumptions he sought to combat. Even at the end, when the film has undercut the anti-Semitic clichés, Rosenthal remains to some degree the outsider. In the idyll on the farm, it is the solidly French Maréchal who has the affair with the blond Elsa. In these scenes Maréchal is filmed working outside on the farm, while Rosenthal, who speaks German, is inside teaching Lotte (and teaching her to count!). He is inside because he is recovering from his twisted ankle, and it is possible that subliminally some viewers might have interpreted this as the representation of another Jewish stereotype. In the Middle Ages Jews were frequently associated with having deformed feet, like the cloven feet of the devil, and by the nineteenth century this had mutated into the idea that limping was a particularly Jewish nervous disorder so that Jews were seen as unfit for military service.[62] Perhaps this idea also explains a line in one earlier version of the script where the actor says of Rosenthal, 'Him an athlete? He was born in Jerusalem.' Maréchal, on the other hand, is the epitome of wholesome French good health. But, of course, Renoir again challenges and works through this stereotype by depicting Rosenthal as a particularly brave soldier obsessed to get back to war.[63]

The intention behind a film may of course be contradicted by its reception. Because many rightwing critics liked other aspects of *La*

Grande Illusion, they sought to interpret the Jewish theme favourably as well. Thus the violently rightwing critic, Lucien Rebatet, whose memoirs written during the Occupation mention his fantasies of machine-gunning Jews, noted that the character of Rosenthal would not harm the anti-Semitic cause since viewers would be reminded, when seeing the film, how different all Jews were in reality from him: he was the exception who proved the rule.[64] In this context, there is a slightly unsettling story recounted by Dalio in his memoirs. While waiting in Lisbon in 1940 for a boat to take him to America, he heard that the Germans had plastered posters of his face around Paris to show the population how to recognise a Jew. Thus, whatever Renoir's intentions in *La Grande Illusion*, or *La Règle du jeu* where Dalio plays a French aristocrat of Jewish origin, Dalio's image was re-appropriated by anti-Semites as the proto-typical image of the Jew (though equally we do not know either how those who saw this propaganda perceived it). Dalio consoled himself with the ironical reflection that 'at least I had star billing on the poster'.[65]

6 Politics: *La Grande Illusion* between the Popular Front and Vichy

The most frequently quoted words from any Renoir film are those uttered by Octave (played by Renoir himself), who shambles through *La Règle du jeu*: 'You see there is one terrible thing in this world, and that is that everyone has their reasons.' The line encapsulates the image of Renoir as a great humanist of world cinema. With the exception of Batala, the capitalist in *Le Crime de Monsieur Lange*, there are no completely black and white characters in Renoir's films. He himself commented: 'In the army with the cavalry, I learned that there are no white horses and no black horses. They always have a number of hairs that are another colour.'[66] On the other hand, Renoir's 1930s films were made when he was strongly involved in leftwing politics. This has prompted some writers to set about historicising his films in order to rescue them from the de-contextualising lyricism of interpreters like Truffaut, who wrote in *Cahiers du cinéma* in 1957 that Renoir's highly political *Le Crime de Monsieur Lange* was the 'most spontaneous' of Renoir's films, 'the most laden with pure truth and beauty, a film I would describe as touched with grace'.[67] Renoir himself certainly later underplayed the extent of his 1930s political commitments, and the Popular Front is barely mentioned in his autobiography.

This contrast between auterist and contextualist interpretations divides critical writing on Renoir and, while one must avoid over-determining the films politically, it is vital to consider the context, and examine the interplay between Renoir's artistic sensibility and his contemporary political choices.[68] Replying to Céline's attack on him, Renoir wrote that 'I was serving nobody' in making the film.[69] This may be strictly speaking true, but his political activities at this time were not casual. He was not just a token participant in political

meetings, and it would have been difficult to display greater commitment to the left short of being a fully paid-up member of the Communist Party. In early 1936, Renoir visited the Soviet Union and he returned enthusiastic. Soon after this, he helped direct the propaganda film, *La Vie est à nous* (1936), for the Communist Party. Immediately after *La Grande Illusion*, he made the *La Marseillaise*, which was conceived to embody the values of the Popular Front. Between March 1937 and October 1938 he had a regular column in the communist newspaper *Ce Soir*. Even if few of his articles were overtly political, some of his pronouncements in the period belie his later reputation of saintly unworldliness. In May 1936, he wrote that most film-makers were 'sons of bourgeois' whose films reflected 'the weaknesses of their decadent class', and he proclaimed the need to give back the cinema to the 'people of France'.[70] In March 1937, he described the Soviet Union as a country where 'filmmakers are free ... not subject to the controls of the market'.[71] In the following year he pilloried Carné's film *Quai des Brumes* as 'good fascist propaganda' because it portrayed 'immoral and corrupt individuals', thereby encouraging people to believe a dictator was required to restore order.[72]

It is not, however, entirely clear what took Renoir into leftwing politics. Certainly it must have been appealing for a somewhat marginal film-maker to find himself celebrated and offered a

La Vie est à nous: French middle-class fascists using models of workers as target practice; real fascists marching

guaranteed publicity machine for his work. Renoir had never enjoyed an easy relationship with producers, and one attraction of the Popular Front may have been its attempt to explore more democratic sources of finance. *La Marseillaise* was intended to be financed by public subscription organised through the trade unions. Furthermore, Renoir's aesthetic preference for filming in depth, linking his characters to each other and to their environment, lent itself precisely to the ideological ambitions of the Popular Front: in his Popular Front films artistic form and political content match perfectly.[73] Renoir may also have been motivated by anti-racism, which was a strong conviction of his at a time when the unemployment caused by the Depression was causing a backlash against foreigners. In 1934 he resigned from the professional association of French film directors when it proposed to impose quotas on foreigners working in the film industry. Several of his articles in *Ce Soir* specifically focused on Nazi racism.[74] He had been very affected by a visit to Berlin with his friend the Jewish film producer Pierre Braumberger when they had witnessed Jews being publically humiliated in the street.

But the Popular Front represented more than a vague opposition to racism, and we need to examine its political agenda more closely to locate its influence on Renoir's 1930s films. The background to the Popular Front was the social distress caused by the onset of the Depression in France. Its catalyst was a violent anti-parliamentary demonstration by allegedly fascist 'Leagues' on 6 February 1934 in Paris's Place de la Concorde opposite the French parliament building. Only a year after Hitler had come to power in Germany, many in France interpreted this riot as an attempted fascist coup. In response, the parties of the left formed an electoral coalition to defend democracy. This was facilitated by the new policy of the French Communist Party (PCF), which previously had advocated an ultra-revolutionary position, refusing alliances with all other parties, on the grounds that there was nothing to choose between fascists and socialists. In the same spirit the Party repudiated bourgeois democracy or support for national defence. But the events of February 1934 alarmed many French communists, and when the Party received a green light from Moscow to change course, its leaders did so enthusiastically. Moscow's new line came about because Stalin, increasingly nervous about Hitler, had no interest in undermining the stability of France, which might be a valuable ally in war against Germany. The PCF now argued that the priority was not revolution but national unity against fascism – internal fascism (the Leagues) and external fascism (Hitler). The Party was willing to support national defence and embrace the symbols of the French Republic: to sing 'La Marseillaise' as well as 'L'Internationale', to wave the tricolour as well as the Red Flag. As part of this strategy, the PCF was ready to welcome even the middle classes and Catholics into the national alliance to defend French democratic institutions. The Popular Front was thus a politically ecumenical movement whose only enemies were the irreducible minority of internal enemies who supported 'fascism'. The Party exploited the iconography of the French Revolution to draw parallels with the present, depicting the aristocratic émigrés of the 1790s as ancestors of fascism.

Popular Front politics were, however, complicated by the fact that some members of the left had different priorities from the PCF. They too wanted to combat internal fascism (the Leagues) because, as pacifists traumatised by the Great War, they viewed it as a militaristic ideology. If, on the other hand, it became necessary to contemplate a war against external fascism (Hitler), the Popular Front would need to choose between two values which had not previously seemed to conflict: pacifism and anti-fascism. The communists had no doubt that they would choose war as a regrettable necessity, but others were less sure. This latent contradiction in Popular Front ideology became increasingly difficult to paper over until it was fully exposed by the Munich agreement of 1938. Many on the left welcomed Munich as an opportunity to avoid a war even at the price of an agreement with Hitler, while others, most notably the communists, vigorously opposed it. At this point, the Popular Front coalition collapsed. The final twist was that some supporters of the Popular Front in

1936 subsequently rallied to the rightwing Vichy regime which took power after France's defeat in 1940 on the grounds that Vichy represented an end to the war.

These ambiguities make it hard to define 'Popular Front cinema'.[75] To return to the case of Renoir, *Toni*, made when the Popular Front was getting under way, reflects the left's concern with the lives of ordinary people, but it was essentially a melodrama which happened to be set among them: it is a social film without politics. Renoir's next film, *Le Crime de Monsieur Lange*, is often seen as the first Popular Front film, celebrating working-class solidarity. But the artisanal community it depicts is rather different from the 1930s French working class, and the evil Batala is more a melodramatic stage villain than a convincing representative of capitalism. The film also has a slight anti-clerical sub-plot – Batala returns dressed up as a priest – which reflects the anarchist sensibility of Jacques Prévert more than anticipating the ecumenicalism of the Popular Front. Prévert and Renoir never made another film together, and Prévert had no sympathy with Renoir's *La Marseillaise*, which is his most explicitly Popular Front work. Although ostensibly about the French Revolution, the film, following the fortunes of a group of revolutionaries marching to Paris in 1792, is less about class conflict than about celebrating the creation of the national community. The only class enemies are the Swiss guard (foreigners) defending the Tuileries Palace, and a few émigrés whom Renoir said were there to incarnate 'this aristocratic spirit which today we call fascist'.[76] As for Renoir's next film, *La Bête humaine*, set among railway workers, its pessimistic ending seems closer to the mood of post-Popular Front disillusion in 1938 than the hopes of 1936.

What of *La Grande Illusion*, which falls in the middle of the period? Although set in the Great War, it does reflect many preoccupations of the 1930s. For example, the derisive comment about Rosenthal coming from 'old Breton aristocracy' echoes rightwing cartoons against Leon Blum in 1936 depicting him in Breton national dress to mock the idea that a Jew could be rooted in the French soil. Another scene which must have resonated in the 1930s is the moment when the prisoners listen to the soldiers exercising in the courtyard. One remarks that there is something seductive about the sound of military music, but Maréchal comments musingly that what bewitches people is the 'sound of marching feet' – surely as much a reference to fascist storm troopers as to militarism in general. It is possible to interpret the escape of Maréchal and Rosenthal as exemplifying the alliance of worker and bourgeois which the Popular Front celebrated: they are the embodiment of the national community forged by the French Revolution. This idea is expressed in the dialogue between de Boëldieu and von Rauffenstein where the former defends the integrity of Maréchal and Rosenthal:

VON RAUFFENSTEIN	You call Maréchal and Rosenthal officers?
DE BOËLDIEU	They are very good soldiers.
VON RAUFFENSTEIN	Yes! The charming legacy of the French Revolution.
DE BOËLDIEU	I am afraid that neither you nor I can do anything to turn the clock back.
VON RAUFFENSTEIN	I do not know who is going to win this war, but I know one thing: however it ends it will be the end of the de Boëldieus and the Rauffensteins.
DE BOËLDIEU	But perhaps there is no need for us.
VON RAUFFENSTEIN	And don't you find that a pity?
DE BOËLDIEU	Perhaps.

This pensive 'perhaps' echoes that of von Rauffenstein in their earlier conversation, and lays bare de Boëldieu's isolation. He resists both von Rauffenstein's and Maréchal's attempts to reach out to him, and remains apart from both of them. Thus, his self-sacrifice appears less a choice of nation over class than a mixture of lassitude, quixotic romanticism and historical realism: dying heroically while simultaneously escaping from a world in which he has no place – like Louis XVI sadly kicking the dead leaves in the Tuileries Gardens in

Renoir's next film. As de Boëldieu tells von Rauffenstein on his deathbed:

DE BOËLDIEU	Of the two of us it isn't I who should complain the most … I'll be finished soon … but you … you haven't finished.
VON RAUFFENSTEIN	Not finished dragging out a useless existence.
DE BOËLDIEU	For a man of the people it's terrible to die in war. For you and me, it was a good solution.

Although one communist critic was not happy with this implication that the nobility had been rendered harmless by the march of time, pointing out that the leader of the Croix de Feu League, Colonel de la Rocque, was such a type,[77] the theme otherwise seems perfectly consonant with the politics of the Popular Front: de Boëldieu's self-sacrifice represents the symbolic triumph of the values of the French Revolution and Republican democracy. Where Renoir muddies the water, however, is in the pathos surrounding de Boëldieu's death: the sombre mood, Kosma's solemn music, the cutting of the geranium. Renoir's fascination with de Boëldieu and von Rauffenstein almost turns them into the heroes of the film. As one writer commented: 'Renoir the artist prevailed over Renoir the ideologue.'[78] With his head Renoir celebrates the march of time, with his heart he seems to regret it, displaying a certain nostalgia for the aristocratic codes of honour, decency and chivalry. These values are on view at the opening of the film when von Rauffenstein, having shot down Maréchal and de Boëldieu, invites them to eat in the German mess. The meal is interrupted when a wreath is brought in commemorating another French airman who has been killed. Von Rauffenstein apologises immediately for this unfortunate 'coincidence', stops the music and everyone stands in silence, after which von Rauffenstein solemnly declares: 'May the earth lie lightly on our brave enemy.' Von Rauffenstein clings on to what he sees as a civilised way of waging war. So too does de Boëldieu. On arrival at the Hallbach camp he protests at the

unceremonious manner in which he is being searched. When told, 'I'm sorry Captain but it our duty to search you ... This is war,' he replies, 'I could not agree with you more, but you can do it politely.'

The film shows none of the horror of the trenches, and, by depicting officers in the air force, it chooses the aspect of the Great War which in the popular imagination still exemplified some of the chivalric traditions of the cavalry. Renoir himself wrote in 1958, when reintroducing the film to a postwar audience: 'In 1914, man's spirit had not yet been falsified by totalitarian religions and racism. In some respects that world war was still a war of respectable people, of well-bred people. I almost say of gentlemen. That does not excuse it. Good manners, even chivalry, do not excuse a massacre.'[79]

By presenting a war of 'gentlemen', Renoir makes it difficult to pin down his views about that thorny issue of pacifism which destroyed the Popular Front. He wrote to the communist Louis Aragon in 1937 that he had made the film to rebut the insinuation that 'everything which is national ('La Marseillaise', the Unknown

Honouring one's enemy

Soldier, in this case prisoners of war) belongs exclusively to the fascists'. But introducing the film to American audiences a year later, he offered a slightly different interpretation: 'I made *La Grande Illusion* because I am a pacifist ... At the time, the usual idea of a pacifist was a coward with long hair yelling from a soapbox and getting hysterical at the sight of a uniform. So I made a pacifist film that is full of admiration for uniforms and escapes.'[80] These statements, tailored tactically for different audiences, are not necessarily contradictory but their emphasis is different: was there not a danger that the viewer would be more seduced by the 'good manners' than horrified by the 'massacre'?

Renoir was as obsessed with avoiding the clichés of pacifism as the clichés of patriotism. His aim was to pay tribute to the simple courage of ordinary men performing their duty without bravado in a way that corresponded to what he remembered of the war. He commented once that he had never met a soldier who talked about abstract ideals. During the discussion between the prisoners on their reasons for escaping no one offers motivation which is conventionally 'patriotic'. De Boëldieu is characteristically flippant: 'As far as I am concerned there is no issue. What is a golf course for? To play golf. A tennis court? To play tennis. A prisoner of war camp is there to escape from.' The teacher is escaping to 'know what's going on back home' (particularly to discover out if his wife is betraying him). The actor is bored. The engineer is motivated by contrariness: 'Ever since they stopped me fighting, I've been dying to get back and fight.' Finally, for Maréchal it is 'just to do like everyone else ... Besides it annoys me to be here while others are getting knocked off.'

Paying homage to the tenacity of ordinary soldiers was a strategy of 'pacifist' films like the 1932 *Les Croix des Bois*, which is closer in spirit to *All Quiet on the Western Front* than it is to *La Grande Illusion*. But even in explicitly pacifist films there was a danger that the message could be blurred: is this 'ordinary heroism' derisory or sublime?[81] It is striking that no character in *La Grande Illusion* questions the war: Maréchal, who begins the film abandoning his plan to see Josephine, ends it by leaving Elsa so he can return to war.

It was this acceptance of war that allowed both communists and conservatives to applaud the film. For conservative critics, the film's message was that war ennobles those who fight in it. The extreme right *L'Action française* claimed that the film showed how 'men in fighting war obey higher laws which transcend them ... War raises men above themselves ... Without war de Boëldieu and Rauffenstein would just be elegant idlers ... Maréchal would just be a dull ordinary bloke living between his aperitif and his bicycle.'[82] For another rightwing paper, *Candide*, the film 'exalts what constitutes for us the essence of intelligent nationalism, the secret link that unites all the men of the same country'. The even more rightwing *Je suis partout* approved 'the simple and virile tone' of a film that avoided the 'tearful sentimentality of Judeo-Parisian cinema'. From the other end of the political spectrum, the communist *L'Humanité* commended the film for its patriotism in slightly different terms: 'Elsa and Maréchal realise that war is not their thing. That it occurs against them, and against their right to happiness ... And yet Maréchal cannot, must not remain under her roof. He must leave. Switzerland and France are calling him.' For the communists there was a contemporary message: workers like Maréchal realised in 1914–18 where their duty lay and the same duty might fall to the workers of France in the 1930s. It was precisely this aspect of the film that caused some reservations on the left. In the satirical *Canard enchaîné*, the pacifist journalist Henri Jeanson wrote: 'Class struggle does not die in war: one only believes one is fighting together because one is sharing the same mud, one is prisoner together ... [but] one is only the unconscious tool of the de Wendels and Schneiders [arms-dealers]. ... War also degrades, my dear Renoir. There are not only gentlemen on the battlefield. There are also murderers and the murdered.'[83]

But whether celebrating or deploring its patriotism, there is a dimension of the film that these critics seem to have ignored, and it is this dimension which strikes us most forcibly today. While *La Grande Illusion* eschews explicit denunciation of war, and presents no scenes of horror, it is all the more effective in its understated depiction of the futility of war. This idea seeps into every crevice of the film, and there is an undertow of exhaustion which becomes increasingly pronounced. The mood in the second camp is darker than the first: the men seem more turned in on themselves. It is the only locale in the film with no scene of people eating together. But already in the first camp, the prisoners are cynical about the absurdities of official propaganda: 'Remember, right at the start, how the Russian steamroller was going to crush them? … And what about Turpinite? With a little bottle as big as a radish we were going to kill off a whole army corps.' Later as the old German ladies in black watch the young German recruits exercising, one remarks to the other: 'the poor young men'. When one German guard asks another why Maréchal is screaming in his cell, the reply is: 'Because the war has been going on too long.' Most poignant of all is the moment when Elsa shows Maréchal the photographs on the wall of her house: 'My husband killed at Verdun … My brothers killed at Liège, Tannenberg, Charleroi. Our greatest victories [and camera pans to the long table with her little girl sitting all alone] … and now the table has become

The pity of war

too big.' The last scene of the farmhouse after Maréchal and Rosenthal's departure is Lotte sitting all alone at the table again.

The only moment of overt heroics in the film is the singing of 'La Marseillaise' (by an English prisoner in drag!) – a scene which surely inspired a similar moment in *Casblanca* five years later. But the futility of this patriotic outburst is underlined later by a poster showing that Douaumont has been retaken by Germans. At this point no one even cares, and one guard remarks to another: 'There can't be much left of it …'

If, then, contemporary French critics were more attuned to the film's patriotism than its pacifism, and if this resonated with the communist conception of the Popular Front, the film has enough pacifism to bring it close also to the spirit of Munich in 1938, which represented the burial of the communist conception of the Popular Front. Indeed, perhaps the film's popularity derived not from the fact that it was a film of the Popular Front – except in reflecting its latent contradictions – but rather that it was an uncanny mirror of the

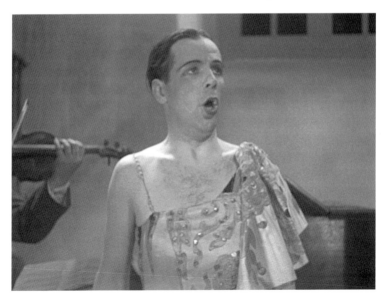

An English prisoner leads the singing of 'La Marseillaise' in *La Grande Illusion*

expectations and anxieties of the French people in the 1930s, oscillating between patriotism and pacifism, duty and exhaustion, resignation to war and the desperate hope that war could be avoided at whatever cost. In that sense the film looks not only back to the Popular Front but also forward to the Vichy regime of the Occupation.

Vichy was not the hijacking of France by a group of 'fascist' collaborators but a regime which crystallised much that France had been in the interwar years. It was led by Marshal Pétain, the most revered French war hero, with the reputation as the general most genuinely concerned about the sufferings of the ordinary soldier. When Pétain signed the Armistice with Germany in June 1940 he presented it as a way of ending useless slaughter in lost war. As if feeling in his bones the country's exhaustion, Pétain offered the French a kind of patriotic absolution for the acceptance of defeat, and his most active supporters were veterans of the First World War

A Czech resistance leader leads the singing of 'La Marseillaise' in *Casablanca*

whom the Vichy regime mobilised to drum up grass-roots support. Vichy's combination of patriotism and Franco-German reconciliation – its 'patriotic pacifism' – seems perfectly anticipated in *La Grande Illusion*. So too were other aspects of the regime's rhetoric. Against what it portrayed as the hollow abstractions of democratic politics, Vichy celebrated the simple virtues of labour, family and the countryside – *travail, famille, patrie* – which are partially embodied in the rural idyll of the final sequences of *La Grande Illusion*, those moments of suspended time embodying the love of man and woman, French and German, against the background of honest rural labour. When Maréchal speaks to the cow on the farm he seems to anticipate the famous Vichy slogan: 'The earth does not lie.'

This is not to say that *La Grande Illusion* is really a proto-'Vichyite' film any more than it is really a 'Popular Front' film – and including a Jew in the national community was completely at odds with Vichy. Rather it is a film suspended between these two seemingly irreconcilable moments of French history, sharing elements of both.

Renoir once said that the only way of creating an artistically successful film was to work in a 'national tradition'. Perhaps it was because he so perfectly achieved this in the *La Grande Illusion* that the result was both so commercially and aesthetically successful. The paradox is that Renoir's seemingly most universal film is also his most French, most rooted in his country's history at a specific historical conjuncture.

What might have been the fates of the film's protagonists if they had lived through to 1940? Rosenthal would have lost his worldly wealth and probably his life. The actor would presumably, without excessive scruples, have continued to sing in Parisian music halls – to houses packed with German soldiers. One can imagine how the anxieties of the dreamy school teacher, always on the margins of life, worried about his wife's infidelities and uneasy with the generosity of Rosenthal, might have led him to support one of the French ultra-collaborationist pro-Nazi organisations, to take revenge on all those people he blamed for his failures. On the other hand, the engineer, who had wanted to escape out of a 'spirit of contradiction', seems a plausible candidate to join that tiny band of people, impervious to the pieties of Marshal Pétain, who set about organising embryonic Resistance groups (where his practical knowledge would have been invaluable). As for Demolder, obsessed with translating Pindar, he would presumably have continued working at his books, deaf to the national drama around him.

What of Maréchal and de Boëldieu? One could certainly imagine the former as an enthusiastic trade union activist during the Popular Front, and later in the communist Resistance. But there is an alternative trajectory which is no less plausible if less obvious. It is possible to envisage him also, with his straightforward dignity, desperately hoping to reconcile his instinctive patriotism and his dislike of war, being drawn into the kind of 'soft' Pétainism which characterised so many First World War veterans, confident that Pétain knew what was best for France, nostalgic about his days on a German farm, and guilty that he had never returned to Elsa. As for de

Boëldieu, he, of course, was dead by the end of the war. But let us imagine von Rauffenstein's shot had only wounded him in the leg – as was intended – and that de Boëldieu had survived the war. One could easily imagine him following a conventional conservative course, a reader of *L'Action française* and a ferocious opponent of communism, welcoming Pétain in 1940 as a saviour of social order. But this does not take enough account of de Boëldieu's mixture of cynical lucidity and quixotic romanticism – qualities more reminiscent of Charles de Gaulle than the average French conservative. In the First World War, Captain de Gaulle had also frequently tried to escape from a prisoner of war camp; he too was notorious for his formality, aloofness and icy contempt, and indeed lecturing in immaculate white gloves (late in life, like de Boëldieu, he also much enjoyed playing patience: it is not a game requiring human interaction). De Gaulle too was member of a caste with no warmth towards Republican democracy or the legacy of the Revolution, but he, like de Boëldieu, had also recognised the inevitability of political change – he was a Republican of reason if not of the heart. Assuming that these imaginary trajectories are right, if we take Maréchal as the hero of the film, perhaps it looks forward to Pétainism; if its hero is de Boëldieu, perhaps it looks forward to Gaullism. All France is there.

7 Afterlives: Escape and Survival

The real afterlives of the film's actors were somewhat different from those we have imagined for the characters they played. Pierre Fresnay continued working in France during the Occupation. His most famous wartime role was in the film *Le Corbeau* and, because this was made under the auspices of the German-financed Continental film company, it landed him briefly in trouble at the Liberation, although he never collaborated in any active way. Marcel Dalio escaped to the USA, where he worked in Hollywood, but other members of his family perished in the camps. Gabin also went to America and then fought with de Gaulle's Free French. Von Stroheim, whose career had been resuscitated by his 1937 visit to France, volunteered for the French army when war broke out, but was refused because of his age (he had also allegedly demanded to serve only in the cavalry – a very von Rauffenstein-like gesture). *La Grande Illusion* had revived his reputation in Hollywood, and once America joined the war there were opportunities to play villainous Prussians in propaganda films. Of course, his most famous postwar role was *Sunset Boulevard* (1950), but he never liked that 'lousy butler part' as he called it, and after it he returned to France where he lived until his death in 1957. In France he was much admired, but he remained partly imprisoned in the role he had played in *La Grande Illusion*, like von Rauffenstein imprisoned in his crippled body. In the 1949 film *Portrait d'un assassin*, where von Stroheim starred with Arletty, he even wore his neck-brace again.

Renoir also spent the war in Hollywood and became an American citizen in 1946. His account of what happened after the defeat is that in the summer of 1940 he was visited by 'two Frenchmen working for Nazi cultural relations' who offered to place any resources at his disposal if continued to make films in France.

To avoid working for the Nazis, Renoir says he decided to leave the country. Probably the truth is slightly more complicated. By 1939, Renoir's commitment to the left was over. *La Règle du jeu* is often viewed as a critique of the decadence of French bourgeois society but it is a not a politically engaged film. Scalded by its failure, Renoir went to Italy at the invitation of the Italian government to make a film of *Tosca*. Accepting such an invitation obviously represented a final repudiation of his former communist sympathies. When war broke out Renoir returned to France to offer his services to the government but was told he could do no better than return to Italy since French policy at this time was to keep Italy out of the war.

After the fall of France, and Italy's last-minute decision to join Germany in the war, Renoir seemed uncertain what to do next. What is striking about his correspondence is his almost total indifference to the defeat. His only thought seems to have been how he could go on making films. In August he was invited to Hollywood by the American director Robert Flaherty. At this time, however, Renoir's preference seems to have continue working on *Tosca* since the Italians had been, he told Flaherty, so 'correct'.[84] Working in Italy after defeat would have acquired a new significance and, luckily for Renoir's reputation, this idea never materialised.

Renoir was also tempted to stay in France partly out of duty and partly in the hope there might be possibilities of making films there. In the summer of 1940 he conceived the project of organising a French rival to Hollywood and to Cinecittà. This was to be a 'cinema village' organised around a church with the aim of defending spiritual values and promoting the formation of an elite. One could hardly imagine a more Vichyite-sounding enterprise.[85] Renoir wrote two sycophantic letters to the Vichy official in charge of censorship, Tixier-Vignancourt, affirming his readiness to participate in the 'renaissance of our national cinema' – 'it is for you to dictate my conduct' – and bemoaning the 'rabble' of his compatriots on the Côte d'Azur – the kind of vocabulary that in 'Vichy-speak' usually designated Jewish film-makers. Two weeks later he wrote to Tixier-Vignancourt soliciting a visa to go to America to make a film about religious missionaries in Brazil. He told Tixier-Vignancourt that this subject would appeal to Marshal Pétain as a way of showing French greatness without falling into 'inopportune' depictions of previous military glory. The film, *Magnificat*, would 'show the slow conquest of spirits by humble and anonymous Frenchmen' and 'reveal the most authentic and moving aspects of the spiritual force of France'. Again one could hardly imagine a theme more in tune with the spirit of Vichy.[86]

Having obtained his visa, Renoir left Marseilles in October to head for the USA via Lisbon. There he delivered a lecture in which, he told Tixier-Vignancourt, he had developed some ideas on the development of a 'latin cinema'.[87] We do not know exactly what he said, but the film historian Claude Beylie has discovered two interviews Renoir gave during his stay in Lisbon, and these did talk about the idea of a 'Latin' cinema to compete with Hollywood: 'the Latins are the great actors of the future. So we must create an intimate commercial and spiritual collaboration among all the peoples of our race.'[88] This 'latin' theme was a favourite Vichy idea about France finding a middle way between Germany and the 'Anglo-Saxons', and it will presumably have also pleased his Salazarist hosts. These remarks later led Henri Jeanson (himself at this time in Paris flirting with collaboration) to claim that Renoir in Lisbon had made anti-Semitic remarks. There is no evidence for this, but certainly Renoir's sensibility at this time seems in phase with Vichy even if he had decided to leave France.

Of course, it was in Renoir's interest not to alienate Vichy if he was to obtain an exit visa and, after leaving France, he did not want to burn his bridges since he was concerned about his son Alain who did not get to the USA until December 1941. Having said that, Renoir never expressed any strong animosity towards Vichy. He had no time for the faction fighting of the French exile community in the USA, and he was no Gaullist. In 1942 he wrote to the novelist Antoine de St Exupéry: 'I detest above all the Gaullists. ... I am happy to break with all the political factions of my ex-country ... I do not like Vichy which is too keen to shoot people, nor de Gaulle who seems too much to want to profit from the situation ... I hate all that politics.'[89] One feels that after 1940, Renoir, like Maréchal on his farm – like Vichy – would have liked nothing better than to escape from history's complications, and cultivate his garden. The problem for him as a film-maker who believed in making films in a national tradition was that although he did eventually return to France and make more films there, long absence had disconnected him from France's present. His American films are not successful except in the eyes of irreducible Renoirphiles, and even when he returned to Europe, his postwar films, with the exception of *The River* (1951), never came near to achieving the sureness of touch of *La Grande Illusion*.

Of course that film lived on. When the film was revived in France after the war, Renoir wrote to Carl Koch: 'What you say to me about *La Grande Illusion* and how the film is almost like a ghost today does not really surprise me at all. You and I put into this story everything we knew about a marvellous civilisation which, alas, belongs today only to the past.'[90] The ghost turned out to have many more lives, and the film's later history is quite a saga, every bit as dramatic as the story told in the film itself. Following the film's journey, as it dodged the crossfire of the censors, takes us from Paris to Berlin to Moscow to Brussels to Toulouse, and finally back to Paris again.

The story of the film's travails started before its release in 1937. The censors had insisted on two minor cuts which marginally blunted its pacifist slant. In the scene where Maréchal is commenting on the haunting sound of marching feet, they cut the end of the sentence where he had originally said that it was 'the same in all armies'.[91] It seems that this was not enough for the Belgian censors and the film was allegedly banned in Belgium where the Prime Minister was Paul-Henri Spaak, brother of its *scénariste* Charles. When war broke out in September 1939, the French authorities became more alert to pacifist readings of the film than patriotic ones, and it was banned in certain regions by some military censors. Once the Vichy regime was installed, the film appeared on a list of 106 films banned in October 1940. It is not clear what aspects of the film incurred official displeasure, but Renoir was still perceived as a film-maker of the left. In general, Vichy preferred escapist films to those with any political message.

In January 1941, the film was also banned by Germany in the Occupied Zone. This is not surprising since when the film came out Goebbels had declared it to be 'cinematographic enemy number one' although it is also said (on what evidence is not clear) that Goering, a former airman, had liked it. The version of the film shown in Germany was heavily cut. Apart from the pro-Jewish angle of the film, it is not clear whether it was the film's patriotism – the 'La Marseillaise' scene cannot have pleased him – or its latent pacifism that Goebbels did not like. This was an issue that divided critics in fascist Italy. One Italian critic saw it as an example of 'Communistoid pacifism' which claimed falsely that patriotism was restricted to an aristocratic class which was doomed to disappear and not shared by the people as a whole. Another denounced it as 'sinister Genevan pacifisim'. But the *Corriere della Sera* judged that the film's pacifist reputation was exaggerated and that the film was 'not at all as dangerous as has been said'; similarly *La Stampa* noted that the film displayed 'ardent exaltation of the most sacred feeling, love of the fatherland'.[92]

One reading of Goebbels' position could be that before 1940 it was the film's pacifism that offended him, and after 1940 (with Germany occupying France) its patriotism. But the film was damned anyway by its sympathetic portrayal of a Jew. After the defeat, not only did the Germans ban the film, but it seems also likely that it was among the films of which Goebbels ordered the original negatives to be seized. The man in charge of German film censorship (*Reichfilmkammer*) in Paris was Frank Hensel. Genuinely passionate about film, Hensel had been appointed by Goebbels to head the

Reichsfilmarchiv in 1934. Two years later, in France, another film addict, Henri Langlois, had set up the *Cinémathèque française* to create a French archive of film. In 1938 when the International Federation of Film Archives (FIAC) was established in Paris, Hensel became its first president. Langlois and Hensel continued to work together in Occupied Paris and the Cinémathèque obtained its first proper premises in 1940 in the same building as the *Reichsfilmkammer*.

The exact relationship between the two men during the war remains obscure, but Langlois lobbied vigorously to save films from destruction, and seems to have found a willing ear in Hensel.[93] It would be somehow appropriate if *La Grande Illusion* was one of the beneficiaries of this example of surreptitious – and, on the part of Langlois, prophylactic – Franco-German collaboration. If there was an order to destroy the original negatives of the film, Hensel ignored it, and one negative was shipped to Berlin instead. None of this was known in 1945, however, and it was assumed that the negative had been destroyed during an allied raid on Paris.

At the Liberation, French film distributors began examining the stock of films banned by the Germans to see what might make money. The producer of *La Grande Illusion* submitted the film to the censors at the start of 1945 – accompanying the demand with a letter showing their irreproachable conduct in the war – but because there were still so many POWs on German soil the authorities felt it would be inappropriate to release the film. Once the war was over and the POWs back, the producers tried again in July 1945. They argued that the film could not be accused of showing a 'good German' since, in the end, von Rauffenstein did kill de Boëldieu. The censors remained unconvinced that the public was ready to accept such a subject.

It was not until the following year that the censors gave their approval. Renoir, still in the USA, instructed Spaak to look after his interests. The film was finally re-released in Paris in August 1946 in a very different climate from 1937. Over 1 million Frenchmen had spent the occupation in German POW camps quite unlike those depicted in the film, and four years of Occupation rendered any favourable depiction of Germans a delicate matter. One critic in the Resistance newspaper *Franc-Tireur* wondered how the public would receive a film depicting events 'which are both so far and so close to those which it has just lived through'. The censors insisted on cuts. These included the scene showing the prisoners receiving copious food parcels from home (seeing prisoners in German camps eating better than most people in liberated France was a provocation too far) and a scene in which Rosenthal hands a German guard a bar of chocolate from his food parcel; the dialogue on the origins of Rosenthal, ending with the mocking remark about old Breton nobility; the kiss between Elsa and Maréchal, and the latter's promise that he would return after the war ('sexual collaboration' was a sensitive issue in 1946). Spaak wrote drily to Renoir: 'Everyone knows that many French prisoners returned from Germany with wife, children, mother-in-law. Only the censors seem ignorant of that … Nothing new on that front!'[94] The poster advertising the film was also different: Dita Parlo's name did not appear, and it depicted a menacing von Stroheim, revolver in hand, about to shoot. Finally, the film was accompanied by a health warning written by Spaak, which appeared at the start: '*La Grande Illusion* depicts a certain aspect of the war of 1914–18. If since the making of this film certain dramatic

Two scenes cut in 1946

The 1937 poster (courtesy of Iconothèque de la Cinémathèque française)

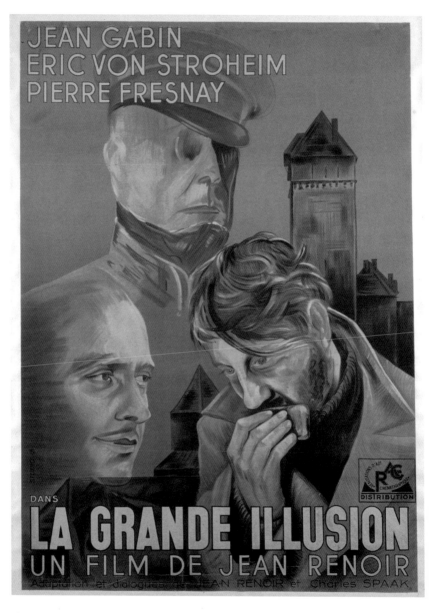

The 1946 poster (courtesy of Iconothèque de la Cinémathèque française)

events have turned the world upside down, the authors do not feel it necessary to correct any of the ideas that they have expressed by basing themselves on historical events.' It ended with Roosevelt's comment that 'all democrats of the world should see this film'.

These precautions were not enough for some critics, especially those associated with the Resistance. The former resister Georges Altman expressed 'disgust' at the favourable portrayal of Germans and the depiction of Jews:

when we are two years away from the Wehrmacht, the SS and gas ovens, one does not have the moral right to invoke art in order to show us Madame Parlo and M. Pierre Fresnay each already collaborating in their own way towards Franco-German friendship ... The Germans are all noble types ... And what about the racism which is so decently portrayed in the person of Gabin who magnanimously forgives the Jewish soldier for being what he is. That is what leads us ever so decently to Auschwitz and Dachau.

He concluded that this was no spectacle to offer 'a people which has only known of Germany the Gestapo, the SS and mass shootings'.[95] The government allowed Prefects to decide if, for reasons of public order, they wished to ban the film in their region. Although Renoir was quoted as saying that it was film about the Germans of 1914 not those of 1945, there was probably also resentment against a man who had not shared the discomforts of the Occupation telling the French what the Germans were really like. It did not help that Fresnay was in bad odour for his conduct during the Occupation.[96] None of this, however, prevented the film again enjoying a major commercial success.

In 1951 Renoir was informed that an original negative of the film had been found by the American army in Munich, where it had been taken by the Germans. Since the RAC had in the meantime sold its rights to a producer who had not paid up, the ownership of the film was in doubt. When Renoir visited Europe for the first time in 1952, the RAC had gone bankrupt and he decided to buy the original

negative, but by then the copy found in Munich had disappeared.
Instead, Renoir set about reconstituting the original from French,
German and American versions which all had cuts in different places.
This was the version re-released in 1958 in a context that could not
have been more different from the immediate postwar years.
This was a period of Franco-German reconciliation with the Treaty
of Rome having been signed in 1957. Renoir, indeed, had even
envisaged a 'European' debut for the film in Charlemagne's former
capital of Aix-la-Chapelle. This did not occur but when the film was
shown in Brussels in September 1958, Renoir presented it as a film
which 'announced the Europe of today, the Europe of the Common
Market'. (The Belgian foreign minister of the time was Paul-Henri
Spaak, now in his postwar incarnation as a supporter of European
unity.)[97] The film opened in Paris in October, and once again it
enjoyed commercial triumph. Parlo's name was back on the poster,
and von Stroheim and Fresnay were side by side with no threatening
revolver to be seen.

The renewed success of *La Grande Illusion* was slightly at odds
with the critical re-evaluation of Renoir taking place at this time.
From the mid-1950s Renoir was becoming a cult figure among the
critics of the *Cahiers du cinéma*, but *La Grande Illusion* was not
their favourite film. Young Turks cannot like the same films as
everybody else. These critics perversely set about rescuing Renoir's
American films from critical oblivion, and their line was that *La
Grande Illusion* was important because it prefigured Renoir's under-
appreciated films of the postwar period. Another critical re-
evaluation occurred when an integral version of *La Règle du jeu* was
re-released in 1965. For film-makers and critics, this cursed film was
a revelation, and it became rapidly celebrated as Renoir's
masterpiece.

The *Cahiers* group was indifferent to politics, or indeed on the
right inasmuch as the left represented the cultural establishment, but
in the 1960s their adulation of Renoir was challenged by a later
generation which had been radicalised by the Algerian War

(1954–62). This new tendency was expressed with some violence in the magazine *Premier Plan* in 1962, where an article argued that *La Grande Illusion* prefigured the reactionary anti-modernism of Renoir's postwar films. The film was accused of displaying 'flag-waving patriotism' and showing only 'rose-tinted war' (*guerre en dentelles*). As the French became increasingly obsessed with the Occupation after 1968, film historians began highlighting the ways in which *La Grande Illusion* anticipated Vichyite values. Marc Ferro discerned latent anti-Semitism in the portrayal of Rosenthal and suggested that the film anticipated Vichy's Anglophobia by portraying the British in a ridiculous light (in the scene where the Maréchal tries to tell British prisoners about the tunnel, he saw it as significant that de Boëldieu, with his perfect English, did not intervene). This reading, although a healthy antidote to the political blindness of the *Cahiers* critics, was ultimately too reductive and paid insufficient attention to the film's ambiguities. And saying that the film portrayed anti-Semitic attitudes did not necessarily make it an anti-Semitic film.[98]

Nonetheless, despite the vagaries of critical reception, the film continued to enjoy general popular success. It became the emblematic Renoir film, screened on French television during a homage to Renoir on his eightieth birthday and again on his death in 1979. It may never have been Renoir's favourite film, but it was the film people remembered him by.

There is one final twist to the film's afterlives which Renoir never lived to witness. In the early 1980s when the Cinémathèque of Toulouse set about cataloguing the original nitrate negatives of a number of films in its possession, it discovered that these included *La Grande Illusion*. It had arrived in France in the 1960s in a series of archival film exchanges with the *Gosfilmfond* archive in Moscow. The film had been taken to Moscow in 1945 by Soviet troops who were occupying the sector of Berlin where the *Reichsarchiv* was located. The Toulouse cinémathèque originally lacked the staff to sort through the films received and the negative mouldered in its basement. After its discovery, months of patient work allowed a new print to be struck from this original negative, and shown for the first time in 1997. This is the film we see today. Having crossed several frontiers, the film had ended its long journey, but Renoir died in the illusion that this negative had been lost for ever.

8 What Illusion(s)?

What, we must finally ask, is the 'Illusion' of the film's title? Although no single 'Rosebud' moment delivers a definitive answer, there are two specific references to 'illusions' in the film. The first occurs in the first camp when the engineer tells Maréchal about the tunnel. Maréchal is sceptical: 'The war will be over before your hole is.' The engineer replies: 'You are under an illusion there.' The second reference occurs just before Maréchal and Rosenthal are about to make their break for freedom across the snow. Again Maréchal is the optimist:

ROSENTHAL   Remember if we get across, you'll being going back to a
             squadron and me to a battery. We've got to fight again.
MARÉCHAL   We've got to finish this bloody war ... let's hope it's the last.
ROSENTHAL   That's an illusion.

Anyone seeing the film in 1937 would have known of the famous book by the British writer Norman Angell, *The Great Illusion*, first published in 1910, and translated into over twenty languages. Angell's argument was that war was an illusion in the sense that a military victory would only be a pyrrhic victory: the 'economic gains of war were illusory'. Awarded the Nobel Peace Prize in 1933, he produced another book in 1938 entitled *The Great Illusion – Now*. By this time he was a strong opponent of appeasement, making it clear he had never intended to write a 'pacifist book in the sense of repudiating defence, or the employment of force to defend it'.[99] We do not know if Angell saw the film, or what he thought about it.

Spaak was the only person involved with in the film who proffered an interpretation of the 'illusion'. For him it was the illusion of friendship, or at least the illusion that friendships formed in war would survive its end.[100] This idea was expressed at the end of his first scenario when Maréchal and Dolette (the prisoner with whom he was originally to have escaped) fail to honour their promise to meet up again at Maxim's after the war. The final scene showed an empty table at Maxim's reserved for two places: neither diner has turned up. In the second scenario this scene was still there but this time only Maréchal has turned up. Of course, quite apart from the fact that the scene was cut, Spaak had no monopoly on interpreting the film's meaning, and we have seen he believed that he had been dispossessed of his own work. Renoir offered another interpretation in 1959: 'it was a title which charmed me a great deal. Its significance only came later ... When I got the film accepted I proposed several titles. *La Grande Illusion* appealed to me above all because it did not really mean anything very precise.'[101]

Probably we should be guided by Renoir and not seek any single interpretation. The film is full of possible illusions: the illusions of friendship and the illusion of peace, the illusion of love (will Maréchal really go back to Elsa?), the illusion that 1914–18 was the last war (an illusion only too clear to those watching in 1937), the illusion of frontiers, the illusion of national reconciliation, the illusion that escape from the camp will necessarily bring happiness (as the teacher says, he has never eaten better than in the camp), the illusions of gender ('Let us dream a bit longer,' says Maréchal), the illusions of race, the illusions of class, the illusions of progress. It is a film where theatricality is never far away: where children play as soldiers, and soldiers play like children; where men dress up as women; where prisoners turn their digging of a tunnel into theatre; where illusion and reality often blur. But, of course, for Renoir illusion and theatricality was part of life. André Bazin suggests that 'the grand illusions are the dreams which help men to live'.[102] It is indeed striking that only one character in the film refuses to accept any illusions and views the world as a meaningless comedy. That character is, of course, de Boëldieu – 'I happen to be a realist,'

Tire au flanc

Boudu sauvé des eaux

Le Déjeuner sur l'herbe

he tells Maréchal when the others are preparing their theatrical entertainment – and he is the only character who dies.

Or is the character we think we are seeing when we watch de Boëldieu himself an illusion? In the first two versions of the scenario, de Boëldieu was to have been called Bois-Le-Dieu, God of the Wood. This might not seem significant except that the image of the nature god playing his panpipes, like de Boëldieu playing his whistle at the end of *La Grande Illusion*, is a recurrent character in Renoir's films. In a short scene in *Tire au flanc* the hero appears as a dancing satyr whose pipes bring a nymph down from heaven. *Boudu sauvé des eaux* opens with a theatrical tableau where the bookseller, Lestingois, playing a pipe, is chasing his maid, both of them dressed in vines and leaves. Then we see him stroking her breast and musing about dancing nude through a moonlight wood like Bacchus. This attempt at seduction is as far as Lestingois gets to breaking out of his bourgeois existence, and it is Boudu who lives out his fantasy of turning order upside down. The figure with the panpipes recurs in *Le Déjeuner sur l'herbe* (1959) in the form of a local peasant whose playing disrupts the solemn meeting of the eugenicist Etienne Alexis, and unleashes erotic energy which turns 'civilised' order upside down. Is it too fanciful to see de Boëldieu as another faded version of these Pan figures, disguised behind the mask of the rigidly conservative military officer who had earlier said 'I hate the sound of

'I hate the sound of pipes' (de Boëldieu)

pipes' but dies playing his pipe, briefly turning the world of the castle upside down and releasing Maréchal and Rosenthal to freedom and love? Perhaps, then, as if scraping off layers from an old master painting, we can see, hidden behind the illusion we have been watching, a film about war or peace or class, another more whimsical, playful and personal film closer to Renoir's earlier preoccupations about the conflict between nature and civilisation, order and freedom, with de Boëldieu as an improbable avatar of Boudu. There are too many illusions, too many games and too many stages in *La Grande Illusion* to be sure we have ever finally revealed its secrets.

Notes

1 After Eisenstein's *Battleship Potemkin*, Chaplin's *Gold Rush*, de Sica's *Bicycle Thieves* and Dreyer's *Passion of Joan of Arc*.

2 Jay Winter, 'Film and the Matrix of Memory', *American Historical Review* vol. 106 no. 3, 2001 pp. 857–64.

3 Jean Renoir, *My Life and My Films* (London: William Collins, 1974), p. 12.

4 Renoir, *My Life*, p. 100.

5 Jean Renoir, *Renoir my Father* (New York: New York Review Books, 2001),

6 Jean Renoir, *The Notebooks of Captain Georges* (London: Collins, 1966), p. 156.

7 'Souvenirs', an article published in *Le Point* December 1938, reprinted in Renoir, *Écrits (1926–1971)* (Paris: Éditions Ramsay, 2006), pp. 53–64 (57).

8 André Bazin, *Jean Renoir* (Paris: Éditions Gérard Lebovici, 1989), pp. 39–40.

9 Susan Hayward and Ginette Vincendeau, *French Film: Texts and Contexts* (London: Routledge, 1990), p. 3.

10 Roger Viry-Babel, *Jean Renoir: Le Jeu et la règle* (Paris: Denoël, 1994), p. 93. This story of a proposed exchange, recounted by Spaak (see Janine Spaak, *Charles Spaak: Mon mari* (Paris: Editions France-Empire, 1977), pp. 143–4), and confirmed by some others, was in fact denied by Renoir in an interview in 1957. See Olivier Curchod, La Grande Illusion (Paris: Nathan, 1994), p. 14, n. 4.

11 Curchod, La Grande Illusion, pp. 36–41 gives a summary of these.

12 Von Stroheim's account was in *Cinémonde* (Christmas 1937), republished in Gérard Vaugeois and Danielle Vallion, La Grande Illusion (Paris: Balland, 1974), p. 210; Renoir's is in *My Life*, p. 166, and *Écrits*, p. 258. There are other versions of

their relations by Spaak in *Paris-Cinéma*, republished by Claude Gauteur, *Jean Renoir: La Double Méprise 1925–1939* (Paris: Editeurs français réunis, 1980), pp. 162–6, and by André Brunelin, *Gabin* (Paris: Robert Laffont, 1987), pp. 214–17, who based his account on the testimony of Jacques Becker.

13 Eugène Lourié, *My Work in Films* (San Diego: Harcourt Brace Ivanovich, 1985), p. 13.

14 The three versions are by Renoir, *My Life*, pp. 137–8; Marcel Dalio, *Mes années folles* (Paris: J.-C.Lattès, 1976), pp. 90–1; Françoise Giroud, *Leçons particulières* (Paris: Fayard, 1990), pp. 78–81. Curchod, La Grande Illusion, 101–2, prints the version of this scene from the second scenario, showing that the song was already there at this stage.

15 Letter quoted in *Archives: Institut Jean Vigo Perpignan. Cinematèque de Toulouse*, 70 (February 1997), p. 16.

16 Renoir in *Cahiers du cinéma*, January 1952, reprinted in *Écrits*, p. 85.

17 Giroud, *Leçons*, p. 79.

18 Renoir, in a 1931 interview quoted in Gauteur, *Jean Renoir*, p. 74.

19 Renoir, *Écrits*, p. 69 [the original source of this article is not provided].

20 Gauteur, *Jean Renoir*, p. 118.

21 Renoir, *My Life*, p. 155.

22 Renoir, *My Life*, pp. 164–5.

23 The farm was found near Neuf Brisach on the Upper Rhine.

24 Renoir, *My Life*, p. 159.

25 Alexander Sesonske, *Jean Renoir: The French Films, 1924–1939* (Cambridge MA: Harvard University Press, 1980), p. 75.

26 Renoir, *My Life*, p. 132 [I have changed the translation].

27 Both quotations in Colin Crisp, *The Classic French Cinema 1930–1960* (Bloomington: Indiana University Press, 1997), p. 312.

28 Quoted in Raymond Durgnat, *Jean Renoir* (London: Studio Vista, 1975), p. 14.

29 Renoir, *Écrits*, p. 59 [from the *Le Point* 1938 interview].

30 Crisp, *Classic French Cinema*, p. 402.

31 Curchod, *La Grande Illusion*, p. 74.

32 Renoir, *My Life*, p. 157.

33 Renoir, *My Life*, p. 152.

34 Lourié, *My Work*, p. 21.

35 Renoir, *My Life*, p. 106.

36 Lourié, *My Work*, p. 21.

37 Sesonske, *Jean Renoir*, p. 319, points out acutely that the playing of this score as von Rauffenstein is about to cut the geranium 'tends to divert the sentimentality of his gesture from the character to the film'.

38 *Renoir on Renoir: Interviews, Essays and Remarks*. (Cambridge: Cambridge University Press, 1989), p. 250; Jean Renoir, *Ma vie et mes films* (Paris: Flammarion, 1974), p. 50 (curiously this phrase is cut from the translation of this book).

39 Renoir, *Écrits*, pp. 125–6.

40 Curchod, La Grande Illusion, pp. 45–51, shows this well.

41 'Le Petit navire' is a traditional French nursery rhyme in which the crew of a ship running out of food draw straws to decide whom they will have to eat. The youngest is chosen but, just as they are deciding whether to fry or fricasee him, a shoal of fish appears and he is saved.

42 Another difference between French and Germans.

43 Genevieve Sellier, 'Charles Spaak ou le réalisme français des années 30–35', *Cinéma 88* no. 299, November 1983.

44 Frenay et Possot, *Pierre Fresnay* (Paris: La Table Ronde, 1975), p. 51.

45 David Thomson, *A Biographical Dictionary of Film* (London: André Deutsch, 1994), p. 626.

46 For example, Renoir, *My Life*, pp. 159–60.

47 Renoir, *Écrits*, p. 257.

48 Quoted in Gauteur, *Jean Renoir*, p. 92.

49 *Renoir on Renoir* 77078 [this is from his interview in the Christmas 1957 issue of *Cahiers du cinéma*. I have slightly changed the translation].

50 In Bazin, *Jean Renoir*, p. 238.

51 Renoir, *My Life*, p. 148.

52 Jean Renoir, *Correspondance 1913–1978* (Paris: Plon, 1998), p. 52.

53 Sesonske, *Jean Renoir*, pp. 317–18.

54 It had been used before, to a lesser extent, in G. W. Pabst's 1931 film about French and German coalminers, *Kamaredenschaft*.

55 Renoir, *Renoir my Father*, pp. 20–1. He had told the story already in an article in 1940, republished in *Le Passé vivant* (Paris: Editions de l'Etoile/Cahier du cinéma, 1989).

56 This version is published in Gérard Vaugeois and Danielle Vallion, *La Grande Illusion* (Paris: Balland, 1974), p. 212.

57 Renoir, *My Life*, p. 90.

58 Sesonske, *Jean Renoir*, p. ix.

59 On Jews in French 1930s cinema, see: Rémy Pithon, 'Le Juif à l'écran en France vers la fin des années trente', *Vingtième siècle* 18, 1988, pp. 89–100; Pierre Sorlin, 'Jewish Images in the French Cinema of the 1930s', *Historical Journal of Film, Radio* *and Television* 1, 1981, pp. 139–50; 'Présence des juifs dans le cinéma français à la veille de la seconde guerre mondiale', in Myriam Yardeni (ed.), *Les Juifs dans l'histoire de France* (Leiden: Brill, 1980), pp. 186–210.

60 Maurice Samuels, 'Renoir's *La Grande Illusion* and the "Jewish Question"', *Historical Reflections* 32, 2006, pp. 165–92 (176).

61 Louis-Georges Céline, *Bagatelles pour un massacre* (Paris: Denoël, 1937), pp. 268–74.

62 Sander Gilman, *The Jew's Body* (New York/London: Routledge, 1991), p. 40.

63 We should remember Renoir had a limp all his life.

64 His review appeared in *L'Action française* under his pseudonym of François Vinneuil on 11 June 1937.

65 Dalio, *Mes années folles*, pp. 147–8.

66 Penelope Gilliat, *Jean Renoir: Essays, Conversations, Reviews* (New York: McGraw, 1975), p. 26.

67 Ginette Vincendeau and Keith Reader, La Vie est à nous: *French Cinema of the Popular Front* (London: BFI, 1986), p. 42.

68 For an excellent introduction to the critical debates, Martin O'Shaughnessy, *Jean Renoir* (Manchester/New York: Manchester University Press, 2000), pp. 30–61.

69 Renoir, *Écrits*, p. 195.

70 Renoir, *Écrits*, pp. 106–7.

71 From an interview in March 1937, quoted in Gauteur, *Jean Renoir*, p. 43

72 Quoted in Gauteur, *Jean Renoir*, p. 184.

73 This point is effectively made by Elizabeth Strebel, 'Renoir and the Popular Front', in K. M. Short (ed.), *Feature Films as History* (London: Croom Helm, 1981), pp. 76–93.

74 Renoir, *Correspondance*, pp. 39–40, on the issue of foreigners working in the French industry.

75 See G. Fofi, 'The Cinema of the Popular Front in France', *Screen* vol. 13 no. 4, pp. 5–57.

76 Quoted in Pascal Ory, 'From Ciné-Liberté to La Marseillaise', in Vincendeau and Reader, La Vie est à nous, pp. 5–36 (22).

77 Georges Sadoul, *Regards*, 10 June 1938, quoted in Curchod, La Grande Illusion, pp. 112–13.

78 Jacques Brunius, *En Marge du Cinéma français* (Paris: Arcane, 1954), pp. 175–6.

79 Renoir, *Écrits*, pp. 331–2.

80 Renoir, *Correspondance*, p. 54 (letter to Aragon, 25 June 1937); *Écrits*, p. 327.

81 Joseph Daniel, *Guerre et cinéma: Grandes illusions et petits soldats 1895–1971* (Paris: Colin, 1972), pp. 120–1.

82 François Vinneuil [pseudonym of Lucien Rebatet], *L'Action française*, 11 June 1937, republished by Curchod, La Grande Illusion, pp. 113–14.

83 For the reviews cited in this paragraph see Daniel, *Guerre et cinéma*, pp. 140–4.

84 Renoir to Flaherty, 8 August 1940, *Correspondance*, p. 81.

85 Pierre Billard, *L'Age classique du cinéma français* (Paris: Flammarion, 1995), pp. 354–5.

86 The letters to Tixier-Vignancourt, dated 14 and 28 August 1940, are in Renoir, *Correspondance*, pp. 85–8.

87 Renoir, *Correspondance*, pp. 97–8.

88 Claude Beylie, 'Jean Renoir, le spectacle, la vie', *Cinéma d'aujourd'hui* no. 2 May/June 1975.

89 Renoir, *Correspondance*, pp. 135–7 (letter of 2 June 1942).

90 Renoir, *Lettres d'Amérique* (Paris: Presses de la Renaissance, 1984), p. 301 (letter of 14 December 1947).

91 Albert Montange, 'Verdun et la Grande Guerre sous le casque de la censure', *Cahiers de Cinémathèque* no. 69, November 1998, p. 73.

92 Bernard Chardère, *Premier Plan* (special issue) no. 22–24, 1962. This special issue on Renoir contains a useful collection of Italian reviews, pp. 247–9.

93 The fullest account is Laurent Mannoni, *Histoire de la cinémathèque française* (Paris: Gallimard, 2006), pp. 78–125.

94 Sylvie Lindeperg, *Les Ecrans de l'Ombre: La Second Geurre mondiale dans la cinéma française (1944–1969)* (Paris: CNRS Editions, 1997), p. 215.

95 Renoir, *Lettres d'Amérique* (Spaak 10/846), p. 222.

96 For the critical reception of the film in 1946 and the quotations in this paragraph, see Lindeperg, *Les Ecrans de l'Ombre*, pp. 209–20; see also *Archives: Institut Jean Vigo*, pp. 27–8.

97 Quoted in Chardère, *Premier Plan*, p. 235.

98 Marc Ferro, *Cinéma et histoire* (Paris: Gallimard, 1993), pp. 184–90. See also a simiilar approach in Francois Garçon, *De Blum à Pétain. Cinéma et société française (1936–1944)* (Paris: Cerf, 1984), pp. 172–4. My own view is that Daniel Serceau is right to argue that one does not 'fight prejudices by refusing to show them'. See his 'A-t-on le droit de montrer un banquier juif au cinéma?', *Cinéma et judéité* (special issue of *CinémAction*) 1986, pp. 142–3.

99 Norman Angell, *The Great Illusion – Now* (London: Penguin, 1938), p. 84.

100 Charles Spaak in *Paris-Cinéma* no. 9/10, December 1945, reproduced in Gauteur, *Jean Renoir*, p. 166.

101 *Bulletin du liaison du ciné-club à Jeunes de l'Academie de Toulouse*, December 1959, p. 9.

102 Bazin, *Renoir*, p. 59.

Credits

La Grande Illusion
France 1937

Directed by
Jean Renoir
Scenario and Dialogue
Charles Spaak
Jean Renoir
Director of Photography
Christian Matras
Art Director
[Eugène] Lourié
Editor
Marguerite Houllé
[-Renoir]
Marthe Huguet
Music by
Joseph Kosma

Production Company
Cinédis presents

Production Manager
Raymond Blondy
Unit Manager
Pierre Blondy
Set Manager
Robert Rips
Location Manager
[Maurice] Barnathan
Assistant Director
Jacques Becker
Continuity
Gourdji [Françoise Giroud]
Camera Operator
Claude Renoir
Camera Assistants
[Jean] Bourgoin
[Ernest] Bourreaud

Stills Photography
Sam Levin
Properties
Alexandre Laurié
[Raymond] Pillon
Costumer
[René] Decrais
Make-up
[Raphael] Raffels
Orchestra
[Emile] Vuillermoz
Music Publisher
Smyth
Prints
Laboratoires Franay-LTC
Saint-Cloud
Sound Recordist
[Joseph] de Bretagne
Lighting Crew
Luxtone
Technical Consultant
Carl Koch
Made at
Paris – Studios – Cinéma
(Hauts-de-Seine, France)

uncredited
Production Company
RAC (Réalisations d'art
cinématographique)
Producers
Albert Pinkevitch
Frank Rollmer
Wardrobe
Suzy Berton
Made at
Studios Éclair (Epinay-
sur-Seine, France)

CAST
Jean Gabin
Lieutenant Maréchal
Dita Parlo
Elsa
Pierre Fresnay
Captain de Boëldieu
Eric [Erich] von Stroheim
Captain von Rauffenstein
[Julien] Carette
Cartier, the actor
[Georges] Péclet
French soldier
Werner Florian
Arthur Krantz
[Jean] Dasté
teacher
[Sylvain] Itkine
Lieutenant Demolder,
Greek teacher
[Gaston] Modot
the engineer
[Marcel] Dalio
Lieutenant Rosenthal

uncredited
Jacques Becker
English officer
Claude Sainval
Captain Ringis
Little Peters
Lotte, Elsa's daughter
Karl Heil
Fortress officer
Carl Koch
von Rauffenstein's batman
Geo Foster
Maison-Neuve

Habib Benglia
Senegalese prisoner
Claude Vernier
Prussian officer
Michel Salina
Albert Brouett

Production Details
Filmed from 3 February–2 April 1937 on location in Neuf-Brisach and at the barracks at Colmar (Haut-Rhin, Alsace) and the Château du Haut-Koenigsbourg (Orschwiller, Bas-Rhin, Alsace) in France. 35mm. Black and white. Mono. 1.37:1

Release Details
French theatrical release by RAC on 8 June 1937. Running time: 3,101 metres/114 minutes (95 minutes after cuts). Re-released in 1946 and 1958.

UK theatrical release by the Film Society (at the Academy Cinema) circa January 1938, BBFC certificate A (passed with cuts). Registered at 10,530 feet (117 minutes 0 seconds) but released at 9,500 feet (106 minutes 33 seconds). Re-released in 1959 by Films de France at 10,170 feet (113 minutes 0 seconds).

Credits compiled by Julian Grainger

Bibliography

Writings by Renoir

Correspondance 1913–1978 (Paris: Plon, 1998).

Écrits (1926–1971) (Paris: Éditions Ramsay, 2006) [a collection of Renoir's journalistic writings].

Lettres d'Amérique (Paris: Presses de la Renaissance, 1984) [a collection of Renoir's letters by Dido Renoir and Alexander Sesonske].

Le Passé vivant (Paris: Editions de l'Etoile/Cahiers du cinéma, 1989).

Ma vie et mes films (Paris: Flammarion, 1974).

My Life and My Films (London: William Collins, 1974).

Renoir my Father (New York: New York Review Books, 2001).

Renoir on Renoir: Interviews, Essays and Remarks (Cambridge: Cambridge University Press, 1989) [a translation of Renoir's *Cahiers du cinéma* interviews].

The Notebooks of Captain Georges (London: Collins, 1966).

Published Scenarios of La Grande Illusion

La Grande Illusion (Paris: Balland, 1974) [produced under the direction of Gerard Vaugeois and Michel Marie, and has a preface by Truffaut].

The English translation by Marianne Alexander and Andrew Sinclair, *La Grande Illusion* (London: Lorrimer Publishing, 1968) is slightly different from the above since comes from a different French edition published in 1964.

Sources on Renoir and his films

Bazin, André, *Jean Renoir* (Paris: Éditions Gérard Lebovici, 1989) [fragments of a never-completed book].

Bertin, Célia, *Jean Renoir* (Paris: Perrin, 1986) [affectionate biography].

Beylie, Claude, 'Jean Renoir, le spectacle, la vie', *Cinéma d'aujourd'hui* no. 2, May/June 1975.

Chardère, Bernard, *Premier Plan* (special issue) no. 22–24, 1962 [important special issue on Renoir].

Durgnat, Raymond, *Jean Renoir* (London: Studio Vista, 1975).

Faulkner, Christopher, *The Social Cinema of Jean Renoir* (Princeton, NJ/Guildford: Princeton University Press, 1986) [intelligent Marxist reading of Renoir].

Gauteur, Claude, *Jean Renoir: La Double Méprise 1925–1939* (Paris: Editeurs Français réunis, 1980) [contains much important primary material not found elsewhere].

Gilliat, Penelope, *Jean Renoir: Essays, Conversations, Reviews* (New York: McGraw, 1975).

Leprohon, Pierre, *Jean Renoir* (New York: Ed Seghers, 1967) [includes some useful extracts].

O'Shaughnessy, Martin, *Jean Renoir* (Manchester/New York: Manchester University Press, 2000) [excellent critical introduction to Renoir].

Philippe, Claude-Jean, *Jean Renoir: Une vie en oeuvres* (Paris: Grasset, 2005) [the most recent biography. Nothing really new].

Poulle, Françis, *Jean Renoir 1938 ou Jean Renoir pour rein: Enquete sur un cineaste* (Paris: Cerf, 1969) [interesting post-1968 critique of Renoir which needs to be used with caution].

Serceau, Daniel, *Jean Renoir, l'insurgé* (Paris: Le Sycomore, 1981) [hard-going auterist interpretation].

Sesonske, Alexander, *Jean Renoir: The French Films, 1924–1939* (Cambridge, MA: Harvard University Press, 1980) [most detailed analysis of the prewar films. Exhaustive].

Viry-Babel, Roger, *Jean Renoir: Le Jeu et la règle* (Paris: Denoël, 1994) [good introduction with lots of illustrations].

Miscellaneous sources

Angell, Norman, *The Great Illusion – Now* (London: Penguin, 1938).

Billard, Pierre, *L'Age classique du cinéma français* (Paris: Flammarion, 1995).

Brunelin, André, *Gabin* (Paris: Robert Laffont, 1987).

Brunius, Jacques, *En Marge du Cinéma français* (Paris: Arcane, 1954).

Céline, Louis-Georges, *Bagatelles pout un massacre* (Paris: Denoël, 1937).

Chirat, Raymond, *Le Cinéma français des années 30* (Paris: Hautier, 1983).

Crisp, Colin, *The Classic French Cinema 1930–1960* (Bloomington: Indiana University Press, 1997).

Daniel, Joseph, *Gierre et cinéma: Grandes illusions et petits soldats 1895–1971* (Paris: Colin, 1972).

Ferro, Marc, *Cinéma et histoire* (Paris: Gallimard, 1993).

Fofi, G., 'The Cinema of the Popular Front in France', *Screen* vol. 13 no. 4, pp. 5–57.

Garçon, Francois, *De Blum à Pétain: Cinéma et société française (1936–1944)* (Paris: Cerf, 1984).

Gilman, Sander, *The Jew's Body* (New York/London: Routledge, 1991).

Hayward, Susan and Ginette Vincendeau, *French Film: Texts and Contexts* (London: Routledge, 1990).

Jeancolas, Jean-Pierre, *15 an d'années trente: Le cinema des Français 1929–1944* (Paris: Stock, 1983).

Lindeperg, Sylvie, *Les Ecrans de l'Ombre: La Second Guerre mondiale dans le cinéma française (1944–1969)* (Paris: CNRS Editions, 1997).

Mannoni, Laurent, *Histoire de la cinémathèque française* (Paris: Gallimard, 2006).

Montange, Albert, 'Verdun et a Grande Guerre sous le casque de la censure', *Cahiers du Cinémathèque* no. 69, November 1998.

Pithon, Rémy, 'Le Juif à l'écran en Fance vers la fin des années trente', *Vingtième siècle* 18, 1988.

'Présence des juifs dans le cinéma français à la veille de la seconde guerre mondiale', in Myriam Yardeni (ed.), *Les Juifs dans l'histoire de France* (Leiden: Brill, 1980).

Sellier, Genevieve, 'Charles Spaak on le réalisme français des années 30–35', *Cinéma 88* no. 299, November 1983.

Serceau, Daniel, 'A-t-on le droit de montrer un banquier juif au cinéma?', *Cinéma et judéité* (special issue of *CinémAction*), 1986, pp. 142–3.

Short, K. M. (ed.), *Feature Films as History* (London: Croom Helm, 1981).

Sorlin, Pierre, 'Jewish Images in the French Cinema of the 1930s', *Historical Journal of Film, Radio and Television* 1, 1981.

Thomson, David, *A Biographical Dictionary of Film* (London: André Deutsch, 1994).

Vincendeau, Ginette and Keith Reader, La Vie est à nous: *French Cinema of the Popular Front* (BFI: London, 1986).

Winter, Jay, 'Film and the Matrix of Memory', *American Historical Review* vol. 106 no. 3, 2001.

Specifically on La Grande Illusion or aspects of it

Curchod, Olivier, La Grande Illusion (Paris: Nathan, 1994).

Special issue of *Archives: Institut Jean Vigo* (Perpignan) 70 (February 1997).

Magny, Joel (ed.), La Grande Illusion (Ministère de la culture. CNC. Dossier 96. 1999).

Reader, Keith, 'If I were a girl – which I am (not): Alain Berliner's *Ma vie en rose* and Jean Renoir's *La Grande Illusion*', *L'Esprit créateur*, vol. 42, (Autumn) 2002, pp. 42–50.

Samuels, Maurice, 'Renoir's *La Grande Illusion* and the "Jewish Question"', *Historical Reflections* 32, 2006.

Vageois, Gérard and Danielle Vallion, La Grande Illusion (Paris: Balland, 1974).

Memoirs of people who worked on the film

Frenay et Possot, *Pierre Fresnay* (Paris: La Table Ronde, 1975).

Lourié, Eugène, *My Work in Films* (San Diego: Harcourt Brace Ivanovich, 1985).

Dalio, Marcel, *Mes années folles* (Paris: J.-C. Lattès, 1976).

Giroud, Françoise, *Leçons particulières* (Paris: Fayard, 1990).

Spaak, Janine, *Charles Spaak: Mon mari* (Paris: Editions France-Empire, 1977).